NEW GRIT

Chris,

Thank you for all the support.
Couldn't have done this thing
without you. Long live the
Hamster Wheel.

Go Bills,

NEW GRIT

STARTUPS IN AMERICA'S
COMEBACK CITIES

ANDY GORDON

NEW DEGREE PRESS

NEW GRIT

Startups in America's Comeback Cities

ISBN   978-1-64137-306-7   Paperback

            978-1-64137-591-7   Ebook

This book is dedicated to my parents who showed me the meaning of selflessness. To my brothers who taught me what grit is all about (whether I knew it or not at the time). To my friends who embody the power of optimism. And to my city that, despite its calloused exterior, exudes all of these traits in spades.

Go Bills.

CONTENTS

—

PROLOGUE

———

This book is a labor of love. A story told out of necessity for cities that are often thought of as second-class, but more honestly, it is told out of appreciation and adoration. I had the joy of collaborating with people who epitomize the spirit of these cities—small business owners, third and fourth generation blue collar workers, and everyday people that make these places special; people who represent the heartbeat of these cities' entrepreneurial future—founders, mentors, supporters, and community leaders; and those who see the opportunity to spark these places to their due resurrection—investment groups, expats who miss their hometowns, and startup-driven economic development experts.

The people and stories shared in this book are undoubtedly a like-minded and eternally optimistic group. Accordingly, there are a few things worth noting before diving into an exploration of promise and potential.

First, it is important to acknowledge the realities facing startup culture in general. Many of the traits exhibited by comeback cities—love, connection, accountability for one's community, and so on—are on display broadly, but that doesn't mean these are magical places where these traits transcend the difficulties of inclusion across startups nationally. Headlines each day will tell you that success in the startup world is not equally accessible to all genders, races, economic backgrounds, and educational backgrounds. When we talk about redevelopment and resurgence in these places, the boom is lopsided. We talk about new tech corridors, new urban centers, and new housing. But in places like Detroit, the city isn't seeing tax dollar benefits from this boom because many of the tech employees live in the suburbs. A boom in many cases, yes, but only for a select and affluent few. It is my hope that the steps laid out in part 4 of this book will help get us there, but let's be clear: there is not substantially more sunshine and roses in comeback cities than elsewhere.

Second, it is crucial to address the implications of the idea of a comeback. In even calling any kind of a renaissance a comeback, I cringe at the idea that we may be disrespecting the people who have been there through the worst of times. The startup community, people suddenly taking interest, and folks now talking about these cities are not here to save. There is no hero complex. Instead, what I aim to do is shine a light. A light on all of the people who never left, those who have struggled to find the work to maintain a life for their loved ones in these cities when future security was anything but a given. It is those people who have never left comeback cities, or those that have come back, that are the reason we see the potential we do in these places.

With all that said, a mind-set of hopefulness is key for the future of these cities, the regions they make up, and the country as a whole. The optimism I hope this book evokes is worth clutching tight.

Let's do this.

PART 1

INTRODUCTION

CHAPTER 1

SKYSCRAPERS

———

"A skyscraper is a boast in glass and steel."

—MASON COOLEY

* * *

I'm trying to think of the last time I went to a new city without stopping to see its biggest structure. Odds are, it's because I'm not terribly original. I've probably just done my minimal internet research before heading out. Google "Things to see in _____," inserting the city of your choice. One of, if not the first thing that pops up will be a building or structure protruding high into the sky. Seriously, try it.

New York? Empire State Building.

London? Big Ben.

Toronto? CN Tower.

Tokyo? Tokyo Skytree

Seattle? Space Needle.

What's my point? Tall buildings are really cool. No doubt about that.

Now, I'm sure you weren't expecting such a groundbreaking, insightful nugget of truth this early on in this book; however, there's plenty more where that came from, so stay with me.

Even if you don't like heights, you would be lying if you said staring up at one from ground level doesn't leave you feeling impressed. Since the first modern skyscrapers were built in New York and Chicago in the nineteenth century, they have given us our favorite skylines, they are—for nonengineers at least—architectural wonders, and they serve as a symbol of status for cities. In a way, the height and look of your city's tallest buildings can be an indicator of how you're doing.

But architects will tell you that the most important element of a tall building that will stand the test of time is its foundation.

This book is about those foundations.

* * *

Take Indianapolis, IN for an example of the power of height. Its tallest building is Salesforce Tower, renovated and renamed in 2017. This forty-nine-floor behemoth is a fitting representation of the city's growth and promising future, as a secondary headquarters for Salesforce, continually ranked as one of the most innovative companies in the world, not to mention their steady annual rise up the Fortune 500 list.

How did Indianapolis—a city that isn't usually top of mind as an up-and-comer to the average person on either coast—get to this point?

Well, they've been a major city due to their location and infrastructure since the industrial revolution. Pair the location and industry infrastructure with strong universities, an abundance of talent, and a growing ecosystem of startup founders, investors, and supporters, and you're beginning to see the picture.

It's "foundation."

While we're considering cities, let's look at these seven:

1. St. Louis, MO
2. Detroit, MI

3. Cleveland, OH
4. Buffalo, NY
5. Pittsburgh, PA
6. Cincinnati, OH
7. Baltimore, MD

What do these cities have in common? They're all second- or third-tier cities that, while having their own distinct character, are not nearly as relevant on a national or international level as cities such as New York, San Francisco, Los Angeles, Washington, Chicago, or a couple dozen others anyone you ask could rattle off. But looking closer, every one of these cities has taken some major hits. Their culture today reflects the complications of a past that continues to define the present.

"For those who were born in the late 1970s and early 1980s, the most vivid past involves the forty years of decline that followed the [mill and plant] closings. Deindustrialization did not displace them. It defined them."[1]

Now let's take a glance up from ground level in one of these cities. Buffalo has a skyline dominated by one building with forty plus floors: One Seneca Tower. The Buffalo skyline would be unrecognizable without it. However, by 2013, it was featured in an article titled *Zombie Towers,* because it

---

1   Linkon, S. 2018. *The Half-life of Deindustrialization.* Ann Arbor: University of Michigan Press, p.4.

had a vacancy rate approaching ninety percent as recently as 2015.[2] Since then, it went up for auction, was purchased, and renovated. The improvements in aesthetics and occupancy are certainly worthy of praise, but this symbol of the city of Buffalo hardly evokes the same kind of optimism and prosperity that Indianapolis's equivalent does. It is essential to note that Buffalo and the other cities mentioned above certainly do have the potential to match this level of positive momentum—and we will spend a sizable portion of the following pages examining that—but they're not there quite yet.

Why is that?

Let's imagine polling a stranger on the street in a major city on the coasts about the difference between Buffalo and Indianapolis. Odds are they won't have much to say on the matter. They may make a comment about geography, with Indianapolis being in the center of the country (relatively) while Buffalo is in close proximity to New York City (try again, folks). For the majority of the U.S. population, the current state of these cities is largely inconsequential. As someone more familiar with these cities, I wouldn't say that this fictional stranger is necessarily wrong. In fact, there are enough similarities between Buffalo and Indianapolis from a

---

2   Campbell-Dollaghan, Kelsey. 2019. "Zombie Towers". *Gizmodo*. https://gizmodo.com/zombie-towers-5-vacant-or-foreclosed-sky-scrapers-acros-1469650045.

historic perspective. But if you look deeper at things such as economic and population trends, or even just take a glance at the skyscrapers, you'll know that Indianapolis has far more momentum to becoming a nationally and internationally relevant city than Buffalo does.

Shouldn't Buffalo be seeing a similar story? After all, both cities do have much of the infrastructure, universities, talent, and growing startup ecosystem mentioned earlier. People from both of these cities have immense and unwavering pride in their roots, grittiness, and a remarkably supportive community around them. The answer, unsatisfying as it may be, involves a little bit of luck and timing.

Admittedly, Indianapolis did not experience the same level of economic and population drop-off that Buffalo did after major industries slowed and left in the 1970s and 1980s, but it's more than that. Indianapolis-borne startup ExactTarget was acquired by Salesforce, leading to a major investment from a major company in the future of this city. Buffalo, on the other hand, has seen entrepreneurial success, but nothing at this transformational scale just yet. While surely luck plays into it, Indianapolis had set itself up to catch this entrepreneurial wave when the opportunity arrived.

Entrepreneurial wave seems like a vague term, so let's unpack it using this Indianapolis example. When ExactTarget was acquired for $2.5 billion, that money could have been put into an Uncle Scrooge McDuck-style vault in which to take a daily money swim or—in keeping with the old cartoon theme—put into a couple giant sacks stamped with a big dollar sign on them and carried off to other cities. Instead, the city has seen a boom of new startups (led by many former ExactTarget employees) and the draw of investment dollars and economic growth.

ExactTarget CEO Scott Dorsey and three partners—two also from ExactTarget—started High Alpha, a venture studio which combines both a startup studio and traditional venture fund. This venture studio focuses on enterprise software startups (like ExactTarget). The studio part of this group helped launch seventeen businesses and High Alpha has invested in forty different companies since its inception. They also raised a second fund of over $100 million in 2018 to continue to launch, scale, and invest in startups in Indianapolis and throughout North America. If all that startup jargon went over your head, it's basically a way to reinvest into other startups in Indianapolis, and attract other venture and angel capital to the city. Because of this reinvestment, the ExactTarget success story was not a one-and-done story. The entrepreneurial wave did not simply retreat back out of Indianapolis; instead, it grew and has helped Indianapolis continue its development as a burgeoning startup hub.[3] This growing hub is now home to other major success stories including Angie's List (acquired by Home Advisor/IAC) and Interactive Intelligence (acquired by Genesys).

* * *

For years, city and regional growth through startup success was thought to be isolated to a few areas (New York City, the Bay Area, Boston, etc.). Although, the past decade or so in particular, has seen a shift in mind-set where this loose model has brought life to areas outside of these hubs—think Austin, TX; Boulder, CO; and Indianapolis, IN. Market dynamics, the unsustainability of concentrated firm generation and associated investment, and ever-changing lifestyle preferences toward urban living without giving up quality of life will continue this trend of entrepreneurial-driven growth in other places.

The race to economic prosperity "elsewhere" is inevitable and cities like Buffalo are equipped with the tools and spirit to drive this prosperity not only locally, but to noncoastal regions that need a resurgence most.

---

3   Hensel, Anna. 2018. "Indianapolis' Highalpha Raises Over $100 Million For Its Enterprise Software-Focused 'Venture Studio'". *Venturebeat.* https://venturebeat.com/2018/07/16/indianapolis-highalpha-raises-over-100-million-for-its-enterprise-software-focused-venture-studio/.

Having grown up a proud native of Buffalo and spending years living in Pittsburgh, PA and Baltimore, MD, I've been surrounded by people waiting for their respective beloved city to make its comeback. It is not out of simple hometown pride that I set out to write this book; rather, it is out of need—a need for an understanding of the benefits that could come with the economic development of these cities and a need for those not standing in these cities to understand their potential.

These cities were the epitome of the American spirit, of American enterprise, and of American innovation. Let me give you a quick rundown of what Buffalo alone was the birthplace of:[4,5,6]

---

4   "Next Things Now: Innovation & Entrepreneurship In Buffalo".
    2019. *YouTube.* https://www.youtube.com/watch?v=E-YgcN-en3U.
5   O'Brien, Barbara, and The News. 2016. "Nation's First
    Gas Well Was Dug In Western New York". *The Buf-
    falo News.* https://buffalonews.com/2016/10/12/
    nations-first-gas-well-dug-buffalos-backyard/.
6   "Imagining The World's First Cancer Center". 2019. *Roswell Park
    Comprehensive Cancer Center.* https://www.roswellpark.org/
    cancertalk/201803/imagining-worlds-first-cancer-center.

Air conditioning	Brainstorming	Skin grafts	First cargo barge
Millard Fillmore	First large-scale hydroelectric power plant	Movie theater	Machine data processing
Country's first daycare program	Windshield wipers	Grover Cleveland	Direct mail
Coffee breaks	Fisher Price toys	Railway suspension bridge	Fingerprint scanner
Business franchising	Electric chair	Jet plane	Fire hydrant system
In-flight simulator	Official furnisher of the White House	American Express	Nineteenth century's largest office building
Country's first park and parkway system	First cancer-only laboratory	Chicken wings	Implantable pacemaker
First building designed by a female architect	Jetpack	Natural gas well	Frank Lloyd Wright's Martin House Complex

Like a Buffalo-borne jetpack or jet plane, the entrepreneurial spirit that once was can undoubtedly take flight again.

It is for this reason that you will not be hearing me talk about the cities this book will focus on—the seven listed earlier: St. Louis, MO; Detroit, MI; Cleveland, OH; Buffalo, NY; Pittsburgh, PA; Cincinnati, OH; and Baltimore, MD—as Rust Belt cities. This terminology was more appropriate twenty or thirty years ago because each city was still scraping the bottom of its potential, referring to the industrial decline shared amongst various cities spanning the Midwest, Great Lakes, and Northeast regions in the late twentieth century. Now, though, these places are at varying points of upswing and warrant a more positive moniker. These seven cities, chosen because they were once top twenty cities in the U.S., but have experienced steady population declines of more than one-third of peak population due to loss of industry, will instead be referred to as comeback cities in the pages to come.

This first criterion that comeback cities were formerly top twenty U.S. cities in population was important because these are cities that not only have the bones to be prosperous again, but they have a culture of carrying a chip on their collective shoulder knowing what once was. A chip can be a compelling character trait for an entrepreneur. Secondly, we are looking only at cities that have faced *massive* population loss. The effects of losing one-third or more of your population (and in the case of St. Louis and Detroit close to two-thirds) are not only physical, but mental. Along with the empty, boarded-up blocks of houses, this loss left the remaining population void of hope and full of feelings of powerlessness.

Remember the words of Sherry Linkon, "Deindustrialization did not displace them. It defined them."

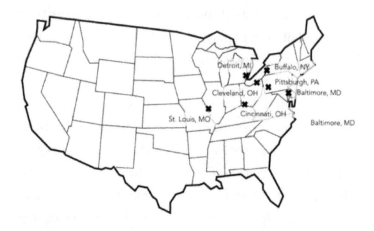

Comeback Cities by the Numbers

City	Peak Population (All in 1950)	Low Population (All in 2010)	Population Loss
St. Louis	856,796	319,294	63%
Detroit	1,849,568	713,777	61%
Cleveland	914,808	396,815	57%
Buffalo	580,132	261,310	55%
Pittsburgh	676,806	305,704	55%
Cincinnati	503,998	296,943	41%
Baltimore	949,708	620,961	35%

* * *

What else do these cities have in common at first glance?
They're passionate about sports.

Take the tortured, but loyal, musings of Ohio native David Giffels in his book, *The Hard Way on Purpose*, regarding hometown hero Lebron James's relationship to the community surrounding the Cleveland Cavaliers after his infamous decision to leave home and bring a title to the Miami Heat:

> *He'll be back. I write these words now on the night that it finally happened: James, the Most Valuable Player, leading the Heat to a decisive championship; I, having immediately turned off the television after the final buzzer, not wanting to watch a celebration that feels bitter and wrong. I look at those words and I really believe them—he will come home—but I know I need to qualify this belief. You come from a misunderstood place and you develop a habit of qualifying everything—and I realize "hope" is the only way to do so, to ultimately believe that that is the force that will conquer, and I curse myself for this, for the goddamned hope of it all.[7]*

As you can tell from that reflection, comeback cities tie much of their emotion to their sports teams because, even when they are unable to compete on the same economic and industrial playing field as "first-tier" cities, they stand a chance to compete and restore their once-constant relevance on the athletic field of competition. For this reason, fans of

---

7   Giffels, David. 2014. *The Hard Way on Purpose*. New York: Scribner.

comeback cities are almost always thought of as some of the most rabid and loyal in the country.

Take, for instance, the Buffalo Bills playoff berth in 2017—the team's first since 1999. It was my first meaningful football game as a Bills fan since I was nine years old. A small victory for a team such as New England or Dallas, this win brought unmatched new life to the Buffalo region. Videos of grown men crying tears of joy (nobody caught me on video, thank goodness) went viral for days. Four hundred fans stood outside at Buffalo Niagara International Airport in two-degree weather at one o'clock in the morning on New Year's Day of 2018 to greet the victorious team plane upon its arrival and show their appreciation—for simply *making* the playoffs. If somehow this community of people were given a Buffalo-borne startup with similar success and applied the same level of rabidity to supporting them, the possibilities are limitless.

This notion is not out of the realm of possibilities. These comeback cities all have the traits to succeed. In fact, they have advantages over many other cities: investment dollars go further; existing industry expertise and Fortune 500 companies; top-rate educational institutions; and finally, the pride, grit, collegiality, and countless other cultural characteristics that make these comeback cities ripe for startup-driven resurgence. But it takes time. And, quite frankly, a little bit of luck.

* * *

On the following pages, I will explain the importance of comeback city redevelopment beyond each city's borders, including the regional and national economic impact, along with social benefits. We will spend much of this book diving into the traits that provide comeback cities their ripeness, using stories and examples from each comeback city throughout. Finally, we will explore some of the additional steps needed to ensure that when timing meets luck, comeback cities will be as prepared as possible to ride their entrepreneurial wave all the way back to prominence.

If you're not yet convinced, let me tell you who exactly should be interested and who will find benefit in reading onward.

- If you are a Rust Belt enthusiast like myself, you will find optimism for the future of this area.
- If you are a politician or community leader, you will find the necessary long-term considerations for your city's future sustained well-being.
- If you work or are interested in economic development, you will find an often forgotten group of cities with considerable untapped potential.

- If you are interested in cities, startups, or startup ecosystem development, you will find an application of many theories to specific cities given their unique traits and cultures.
- If you are a millennial who cannot fathom the possibility of owning a home and having a good quality of life in your current city, you will find promise in places you had not considered.
- Finally, if you are a fan of comebacks and underdogs, or are simply wondering how a community can dig itself out of a hole, look no further.

Like so many of us who have committed to proving to ourselves that we can get up off the mat, these comeback cities are determined to prove their supporters right and their naysayers wrong. They are so immensely confident in the spirit and resources of their city that their resurgence is inevitable.

They're not hoping for a comeback, they're waiting.

CHAPTER 2

IMPORTANCE OF COMEBACK CITIES

———

Pick a random person from one of the comeback cities and ask them why they care about any kind of economic revival in their city and they will rattle off a dozen reasons in an instant. Shoot, instead of rattling off my own dozen, I decided to write a book about it. I had *that* much to say.

Even those who have become expats and do not plan on returning to their hometown will feel strongly about the importance of resurgence because of their deep roots. Pose that same question to someone—nay, anyone—unaffiliated with these cities, though, and you might get nothing in return. For the majority of the U.S. population, the post-deindustrialized state of these cities is all they've ever known and their fate has largely been an afterthought for anyone outside of their city's borders.

I don't blame Californians who don't have much concern on the state of affairs in Cincinnati or Baltimore. I get it. Why should they care?

The answer is multifaceted and complex. It requires that the individual take a broader vision of their country, region, city, and society as a whole.

The arguments we will cover include:

- National economic benefits
- Regional economic benefits
- Small town economic benefits
- Social and political benefits
- Why redeveloping comeback cities > developing new cities from scratch

* * *

The most well-known group examining this very question to date has been Revolution's Rise of the Rest Seed Fund (ROTR). Revolution, a venture capital firm based out of Washington, DC was founded by America Online (AOL) co-founder Steve Case in 2005. Case launched the Rise of the Rest initiative in 2014, aimed at finding startups outside of New York City, Boston, and Silicon Valley which at the time of ROTR's launch received an astounding three-quarters of all venture funding. This number has since increased to nearly eighty percent as of 2019.[8]

The ROTR Seed Fund was born out of the initiative and was launched in 2017. By taking bus tours to the cities in the "rest" of the country to hear pitches from local founders and invest in their startups, the ROTR team seeks to seize an opportunity in finding undervalued companies that will be key to the integration of technology and industries such as agriculture, manufacturing, and medicine in the future.

According to Case, "Not taking advantage of the industry expertise of places like the Cleveland Clinic in Cleveland, Johns Hopkins in Baltimore, or the robotics expertise in Pittsburgh will likely result in missing the opportunity for America to lead."

At the same time, it is as much about solving a problem as it is seizing an opportunity.

When asked to ponder the importance of these cities, Case explained, "Why do these comeback cities matter? If we don't create a more inclusive innovation economy, more jobs, and

---

8   "15 Charts That Show US VC Could Break Multiple Records In 2019". 2019. *Pitchbook*. https://pitchbook.com/news/articles/15-charts-that-show-us-vc-could-break-multiple-records-in-2019.

even more hope, the divides we have now could get worse and have the potential to be catastrophic."

Continuing to trend towards the concentration of new ideas, innovations, and technology in a select few places around the country is unsustainable, simply put.

Looking at economic impacts on a national scale is the broadest way to see the importance of comeback city resurgence. Brookings has done two versions of an in-depth study on cities similar to comeback cities, outlined most recently in a 2018 report titled "Renewing America's Economic Promise Through Older Industrial Cities." In it, they build on the main premise of ROTR's thesis: "A more balanced urban system, in which small and medium-sized cities play a fundamental role in the mobilization of local assets to exploit local synergies, seems to be a better strategy than intense urban concentration."[9]

Comeback cities will be at the forefront of cities that will play this fundamental role in a more balanced urban system.

---

9   Berube, Alan & Murray, Cecile. "Renewing America's economic promise through Older Industrial Cities". 2018. *Brookings*. https://www.brookings.edu/wp-content/uploads/2018/04/2018-04_brookings-metro_older-industrial-cities_full-report-berube_murray_-final-version_af4-18.pdf.

Investing in a diverse array of urban centers is an important safeguard against the ever-present uncertainty our world faces in the form of climate change, domestic divides, international conflicts, and technological disruption. What this boils down to is that the spread of opportunity to places like comeback cities will be essential to individual and societal well-being.

The American dream so many politicians refer to is increasingly elusive for the average citizen because more individuals are planting roots (or at least trying to plant roots) in a concentration of a few major urban areas. This is largely to do with the fact that economic success is increasingly concentrated to a select few urban areas. The top twenty-five metro areas in the U.S. (out of a total of 384) accounted for more than half of the $19.5 trillion national gross domestic product (GDP) in 2017.[10]

In addition to the material desires and financial security of this American dream, there is a desire for a real sense of community that is difficult to find in the masses of the country's biggest metropolises. Comeback cities can provide a realistic avenue to the best of both worlds—the prospect of the American dream *and* a thriving urban area with all the positives that come with living in a city.

---

10 "GDP By Metropolitan Area". 2019. *U.S. Bureau of Economic Analysis (BEA)*. https://www.bea.gov/data/gdp/gdp-metropolitan-area.

* * *

One of the effects of the comeback cities' former size and prominence is that they have the ability to once again become centerpoints from which a hub and spoke model can help revitalize not only the cities themselves, but the rest of the important surrounding regions as well. The hub and spoke model is one which would take advantage of each comeback city as a nucleus contributing to the economic development of nearby towns, cities, and rural regions like the center of a wheel with its economic impacts reaching out to proximate locales via spokes.

When looking at entrepreneurship as a driver, this regional perspective is even more important because possible relationships between neighboring cities and towns amplify the reach of new ideas. From a cultural perspective, many comeback city neighbors are fiercely loyal to their city above all else. Despite this, they are willing to put aside rivalries with neighboring cities or states to grow together.

Take Detroit, for instance.

Detroit natives are likely to consider themselves Detroiters, Michiganders, and Midwesterners in that order. Despite the obvious cultural differences between urban Detroit and its college-town neighbor Ann Arbor, entrepreneurs from both locations have begun to put their Michigan ties at the fore-front in creating a collaborative regional ecosystem. At the same time, there is room for improvement. When ROTR investors visited Ann Arbor in 2017, *Hillbilly Elegy: A Memoir of a Family and Culture in Crisis* author and ROTR Seed Fund Managing Partner, J.D. Vance, noted "There is a tension in how you brand the relationship between Ann Arbor and Detroit...that needs to be fixed and the two areas need to be viewed together more on a national scale."[11] There is still work to be done to reap the benefits of this proximity.

Dan Gilbert, Quicken Loans chairman who moved the company to Detroit in 2005, felt a similar tension upon making that move, but noted, "Now we're building connections and creating networks linking the whole region."[12] These connections help not only in terms of creating ideas and partnerships, but also by drawing talent and investment. With the small, but growing entrepreneurial communities such as Grand Rapids, Lansing, and Marquette, a wider Michigan entrepreneurial region has the potential to reach even greater heights in the future. Helping Detroit to continue its climb

---

11   "Ann Arbor, Detroit Must Work Together to Further Investment, Rise Of The Rest Panel Says". 2017. *Crain's Detroit Business.* https://www.crainsdetroit.com/article/20171012/news/641841/ann-arbor-detroit-must-work-together-to-further-investment-rise-of-the.

12   Ibid.

out of the hole that had been dug will also give a leg up to each of these neighboring spots.

The beauty of comeback cities is their geographic proximity to so many other growing and—in some cases—thriving entrepreneurial towns and cities to build out these regional ecosystems, referred to as adjacent markets. Like the potential that lies in the Detroit-Ann Arbor relationship, each of the comeback cities has multiple cities and entrepreneurship centers within a two-hour drive:

- Baltimore: Washington, DC; Philadelphia, PA; Harrisburg, PA
- Buffalo: Hamilton, ON; Rochester, NY; Erie, PA; Toronto, ON; Kitchener-Waterloo, ON
- Cincinnati: Louisville, KY; Lexington, KY; Dayton, OH; Indianapolis, IN; Columbus, OH
- Cleveland: Youngstown, OH; Erie, PA; Akron, OH; Toledo, OH
- Detroit: Ann Arbor, MI; Toledo, OH; Lansing, MI; Bowling Green, OH
- Pittsburgh: Morgantown, WV; Youngstown, OH; Akron, OH
- St. Louis: Springfield, IL; Columbia, MO

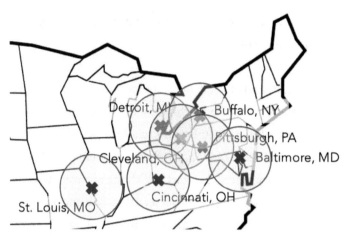

Figure: Areas within a 100-mile radius of comeback cities.

In a similar state of work-in-progress to the Detroit-Ann Arbor regional relationship, Baltimore has already yielded considerable benefits from its proximity to the nation's capital, planting the seeds to become a cybersecurity technology hub.

One of the key components that helped this come to be is Baltimore taking advantage of Washington's deep pools of cybersecurity talent and technology, especially in the Northern Virginia and Maryland suburbs because of the concentration of federal government work there. A 2017 assessment of Washington's cybersecurity industry reports an astounding 858 businesses in the region. More than half of the companies are either in Fairfax County, VA or Montgomery County, MD—both Washington suburbs. Ninety-four percent of area cybersecurity firms reported working with government clients.[13]

Baltimore, in and of itself, does not have nearly the cybersecurity resources that the Washington metropolitan area does, but because of its proximity and relative bang-for-your-investment-buck, cost of living, and other benefits, has found an opportunity to reinvent itself. With the apparent need to spur commercial-focused cybersecurity, Baltimore is well positioned to utilize abundant resources and be the driver of this effort.

Comeback cities as a group can take advantage of their relative proximity to other growing and thriving communities to accelerate their own growth, and the cycle of regional prosperity has the potential to spiral and further its geographic reach.

* * *

Recognizing the proximity benefits to nearby cities is easy enough to understand based on the similar resource needs

---

13   Aberman, Jonathan, Erran Carmel, and Bini Byambasuren. 2019. "Cybersecurity Startup Founders in Greater Washington, DC". *Kogod School of Business.* https://www.american.edu/kogod/research/publications/upload/cyber_founders_report.pdf.

between cities striving for similar economic conditions. Baltimore and Washington are both major cities, after all.

It is admittedly a little bit more complicated to see the direct benefits of a boom in any of the comeback cities yielding rewards for more remote and rural locations throughout the Heartland and Rust Belt. The geographic area surrounding the seven comeback cities is one that has seen a stark decline in a number of economic and well-being indicators, with studies reframing these regions as belts of desperation, unhappiness, and worry.[14]

Rural economic development consultant Erik Pages noted that there are three different types of rural or small-town areas:

1. Scenic—those that have a natural draw to them, often due to some kind of natural beauty or attraction (e.g., Jackson, WY; Kennebunkport, ME; the Finger Lakes region of Western New York)
2. Non-scenic—those that do not have any kind of natural or tourist attraction (e.g., most of the struggling towns whose name you likely wouldn't recognize)

---

14 Florida, Richard. 2017. "Mapping America's 'Desperation Gap'". *Citylab*. https://www.citylab.com/life/2017/11/the-geography-of-desperation/545459/.

3. Urban links—those that have a close geographic or economic link to a large urban center (e.g., Cranberry Township, PA; Loudoun County, VA)

Many of the surrounding areas to comeback cities would unfortunately fall into that second category. They are not scenic attractions, but there is hope that they can benefit from being urban links in the future. In Western Pennsylvania, for instance, there are countless smaller steel towns along Pittsburgh's three rivers that include the likes of Braddock, Duquesne, Rankin, and Aliquippa, all of which were impacted in much the same way as the Steel City itself when steel mills shut down and citizens were left to fend for their own futures.

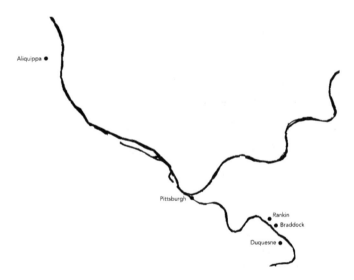

A 2015 exposé looked at the plight of Aliquippa specifically, which had not seen any reinvestment or upswing to speak of like neighboring Pittsburgh had. The town saw its peak in the 1940s with a population of more than 27,000 with nearly 9,000 people employed at the Aliquippa Works. In 1984, LTV Corp. closed most of the Aliquippa Works, which led to the laying off of about 8,000 employees. From there, the town saw a sharp decline to where today's population sits at about 9,000.

Award-winning documentary photographer Pete Marovich who set out to document Aliquippa's plight, described his thoughts on what, if any, hope Aliquippa had for the future:

> *Some of the old-timers still long for the good old days and talk about how things will be when the mill comes back. But most people realize those days are gone. Most of the storefronts along the main thoroughfare of Franklin Avenue are still boarded up, and there are a lot of empty lots between buildings. Recently the city was able to attract United States Gypsum to the area, and they built a plant along the Ohio River located on part of what was the former J&L site. There is still a lot of land on the old mill site—land that sits on the river and a rail line. It is a prime spot for some new industry, such as a car manufacturer. The residents understand that the city needs to attract more businesses and jobs if Aliquippa*

is to fully recover. New businesses will raise the tax base and provide funds to rebuild the decaying infrastructure. The people of Aliquippa are strong, resilient and proud of their heritage. They are doing their best in difficult times, and they are continuing to press forward.[15]

People in towns like Aliquippa are not going to stop pressing forward. It's just not how they operate. It is not surprising then, that they do not expect a revival in a place like Pittsburgh to lift them up and make lasting improvements to the economy of their particular town. Sure, a new business could open and create a few new jobs, but that is not sustained progress. Although complete revival of a city like Aliquippa simply due to a Pittsburgh resurgence is not realistic, the hub and spoke effect of sustained success in Pittsburgh *can* yield tangible benefits for people who consider their towns to be forgotten. The steel mills are not going to reopen and return things to their former state, but the spread of jobs to the suburbs of Pittsburgh and beyond has the potential to bring commutable opportunity closer to places like Aliquippa.

There is hope that the existing connections that the surrounding suburban and rural regions have to nearby comeback

15   Crowder, Nicole. 2015. "The Life and Slow Death of a Former Pennsylvania Steel Town". *Washington Post.* https://www.washingtonpost.com/news/in-sight/wp/2015/11/11/part-ii-the-life-and-slow-death-of-a-former-pennsylvania-steel-town/?noredirect=on.

cities will allow for the spread of spokes from each of them as a hub. The development of these cities in bands of down-trodden nonurban areas can trickle outward, and whether or not it is a total return to the glory days of the past, there can be marked improvement from recent trends.

* * *

The region that comeback cities occupy has been the focus of considerable discussion around social and political divides over the past decade. According to a report from the Brookings Institution:

> *Regional inequalities in the United States today have undoubtedly deepened political divisions that threaten America's social cohesion and democratic institutions[...] the moments in modern history when growth was not widely shared were precisely those times when political and social progress stalled. Growing inequality and a lack of overarching economic possibility and opportunity in many of our communities has provided fertile ground for growing resentment across racial, ethnic, class, and geographic lines.*[16]

---

16 Berube, Alan & Murray, Cecile. "Renewing America's economic promise through Older Industrial Cities". 2018. *Brookings.* https://www.brookings.edu/wp-content/uploads/2018/04/2018-04_brookings-metro_older-industrial-cities_full-report-berube_murray_-final-version_af4-18.pdf.

Beyond the economic scope of comeback city resurgence, ancillary social and political benefits are huge. We'll all be better off. There are limitless examples.

If we think about comeback city resurgence as a mechanism to reducing both regional and local inequalities in access to economic well-being, there are fundamental health benefits. For instance, the effects of stresses associated with inequality and the resulting poverty include delayed development of adolescent brains around learning and executive function, a challenge to be improved upon by reducing that inequality.[17] A political impact of continued high levels of inequality is that it leads to less involvement in civic and political activities.[18] We won't dive into the innumerable other examples—there are many more expert and fully-wrought pieces on the topic already out there—but these noneconomic impacts further disparities between thriving regions and those left behind.

Politically, the U.S. is more divided between urban and rural, left and right, rich and poor, than anyone living today has

17 *"Unequal Stress: How Poverty is Toxic for Children's Brains".* 2016. Mailman School of Public Health. *https://www.mailman.columbia.edu/public-health-now/news/unequal-stress-how-poverty-toxic-children%E2%80%99s-brains.*

18 Lancee, Bram, and Herman G. Van de Werfhorst. 2012. "Income Inequality And Participation: A Comparison Of 24 European Countries". Social Science Research 41 (5): 1166-1178. doi:10.1016/j.ssresearch.2012.04.005.

seen. Or, at the very least, those divides are more readily observable than ever before. Whether you're driving down a two-lane road carving through the mountains of Central PA, or cruising down your Twitter timeline, you see it. It is on handmade front lawn signs and borderline unreadable tweet threads. By sheer common sense, the redevelopment of smaller cities and their surrounding areas would be able to bridge this gap in ways that further concentrated urban development would only exacerbate.

* * *

We have covered the national, regional, and local economic benefits of comeback city redevelopment. We have touched on the political and social benefits. But there is still one common question left to cover in terms of why these cities are worth redeveloping. It is one I have been asked a number of times:

Why should we try to rebuild cities that have more or less fallen apart when we could, instead, try to develop new cities from scratch without worrying about any existing mess to clean up?

I would never be foolish enough to insist that comeback city redevelopment is the only—or even the absolute best—path towards a more prosperous and, frankly, happy nation.

According to author and journalist Monte Reel, the desire to build cities from scratch has been omnipresent for as long as humans can remember:

> *Embedded in the cerebral folds of every city planner who's ever lived, there's a cluster of neurons that lights up like Las Vegas when confronted with the possibility of a blank slate. It started with Hippodamus, the man Aristotle claimed was the father of urban planning. When the Persians destroyed his hometown of Miletus, Hippodamus discovered a bright side to catastrophe: The attackers had erased all the regrettable improvisations that, over the centuries, had made a mess of the place. Tasked with rebuilding, he seized his chance to impose order upon chaos. And so, the concept of the urban grid was born[.] Ever since, the dream of carte blanche has proved an all-but-irresistible seduction. Leonardo da Vinci drafted detailed sketches of an "ideal city" after the plague ravaged Milan, and a few hundred years later, Frank Lloyd Wright designed a metropolis that solved the problem of vehicular congestion via a network of helicopter taxis.[19]*

19 Reel, Monte. 2018. "The Irresistible Urge to Build Cities from Scratch". *Bloomberg Businessweek.* https://www.bloomberg.com/news/features/2018-11-02/the-irresistible-urge-to-build-cities-from-scratch.

Don't get me wrong. I see the appeal in a blank slate as much as anyone else. But seeing this appeal doesn't take away from the other appeal of reimagining, adapting, and rebuilding the cities upon which much of American history was built.

To disregard this comeback city resurgence in favor of a blank slate would ignore the assets—both physical and human— that these cities have to offer. Many of them were built where they are due to their useful geographic location or abundance of natural resources. They all were built upon one or more particular niche industries, for which generations of their inhabitants developed irreplaceable skill sets and know-how. Beyond the physical and knowledge-based advantages of rebuilding these formerly prosperous cities, it would be decidedly impossible to match the spirit and the culture of these cities from a blank slate.

While new cities can and should be developed through-out America as part of our quest to prosper together, these comeback cities can and should also be redeveloped, for the impacts of such a revival on the local and national econo-mies, and the associated social and political effects, would be unquestionably positive.

* * *

So, as a newly christened comeback city champion, let's summarize your talking points when you find yourself in a heated debate with a fictitious stranger from New York City or San Francisco on the topic:

- Continued concentration of wealth and population in a select few cities is not only economically unsustainable, but it puts us at a disadvantage to other leading economies.
- Comeback city redevelopment has hub and spoke benefits to nearby cities and rural areas, many of which have been hit hardest by economic and health crises.
- The toxic levels of social and political divide can be bridged by the development of comeback cities and shared prosperity across these imaginary divides.
- Rather than build new cities from scratch, comeback cities have centuries-long assets in their people and infrastructure that make them ripe for a quick comeback.
- If all four above points don't do the trick, take a deep breath, walk away, and smile knowing that you don't need their belief to know that a comeback is on the horizon.

CHAPTER 3

WHY STARTUPS?

———

Now that we have covered why these cities matter from an outside perspective, why are we focusing this book on entrepreneurship, and more specifically startups?

To begin, let's define what exactly we mean by entrepreneurship. You can get as poetic as to say that it is a spirit or an energy. You can get as lofty as to say it is the process of creating solutions to the world's problems. For our purposes, we will consider it to be the creation of new firms, inclusive of everything from hyper growth startups to mom and pop shops on Main Street. An analysis of Rust Belt metropolitan statistical areas (MSAs) looking at employment and wages shows that high-growth MSAs tend to be comprised of firms that are larger and younger, while MSAs with less growth tend to have firms that are smaller and older.[20] Accordingly,

---

20 Faberman, R. Jason. 2002. "Job Flows and Labor Dynamics in the U.S. Rust Belt". *Monthly Labor Review.*

many stories throughout this book will be focused on start-ups—those companies with high-growth potential—because of their ability to impact a local and regional economy, as well as their applicability as a storytelling mechanism.

The most obvious reason entrepreneurship is so important to city growth and redevelopment is because, at its core, it is job creation. From nothing, entrepreneurs are able to create employment for their workers. Without the creation of new firms, there would be virtually no net job growth in the U.S. economy and new firms alone account for nearly twenty percent of gross job creation.[21,22] The key here for startups is that this job growth is rooted job growth. It is not a quick couple jobs that may or may not be there in a few years. These are companies and jobs that can anchor a community.

This should not really be news, but if we skated by this inherent and potentially obvious benefit, the answer to the question of "Why Startups?" would be incomplete.

While this is undeniably good in and of itself, there are additional benefits to the greater community other than sheer employment numbers. New companies create competition,

21 Kane, Tim. 2010. "The Importance of Startups in Job Creation and Job Destruction". Kauffman Foundation Research Series: Firm Formation and Economic Growth. *Kauffman Foundation.*

22 "The Importance of Young Firms for Economic Growth". 2014. *Entrepreneurship Policy Digest.* Kauffman Foundation.

innovation, and ecosystem-wide advancement—from partnerships to events and culture. There are also collateral
advantages gained when new companies find success, including the attention of investors for new projects and evolving
local policies to meet the needs of a growing entrepreneurial
ecosystem.

To me, even more important than creating jobs is the notion
that entrepreneurship is the only economic development
strategy available to *all* communities. It is a means to self-ac-
tualization beyond just having a job. Ultimately, happy and
fulfilled lives accessible to all should be the goal, not simply
job creation. Through entrepreneurship, this can be achieved.

* * *

In the coming pages, we'll cover some of the characteristics of comeback cities that make them particularly fertile
ground for an entrepreneurship-driven comeback, but it is
important to first note how entrepreneurship has lacked in
these cities since their industrial decline, all the more reason
that bolstering this maker mentality may be just the ticket to
help reimagine and regain the glory of the past.

In essence, entrepreneurship will be one of the key drivers of
economic success for these cities in the future because, beginning in the era immediately following industrial decline,

these cities were at a near-zero baseline for entrepreneurial know-how compared to other cities that had not developed in the same way around a few industry-specific employers.

Renowned urban and regional economist Benjamin Chinitz originally looked into the topic of a city's industrial focus and its effect on entrepreneurialism, innovation, and thus long-term growth.

According to modern economists Edward Glaeser, Sari Kerr, and William Kerr:

> Chinitz claimed that Pittsburgh's dearth of entrepreneurs in the 1950s reflected its historical concentration in steel, which in turn reflected proximity to large deposits of coal and iron ore. The steel industry has significant returns to scale, and Chinitz argued that its presence crowded out more entrepreneurial activities. This left Pittsburgh with an abundance of company men but few entrepreneurs. Moreover, Chinitz emphasized how this dampening of entrepreneurship comes through both static factors (e.g., access to inputs for new businesses) and dynamic factors (e.g., the transmission of skills and attitudes from parents to children). Chinitz's hypothesis was, in a sense, an early conception of the natural resource curse, which in this case, operates through large, resource-intensive activities

crowding out the entrepreneurial activity which generates long-term growth.[23]

That's a lot to chew on, huh? But it's an interesting hypothesis.

Think about comeback cities who relied for more than half of a century on one or two primary manufacturing industries. For instance, if steel was the only game in town, not only would it be nearly impossible for someone to start a business in that industry, but it also incentivized the population to come work for the major employers, rather than starting a company in a different industry on their own. Because this stable cycle persisted for generations, parents often encouraged children to seek the same type of stable employment. Not only did these few major employers promote stability over all else, but they failed to elevate wages because of a lack of competition for talent. Because the industries of choice were raw material and resource intensive, the churning out of intellectual talent did not occur like it did in less labor-focused industries.

Chinitz's famous article from 1961, *Contrasts in Agglomeration: New York and Pittsburgh,* uses the two cities to make his

---

23   Glaeser, Edward, Sari Kerr, and William Kerr. 2012. "Entrepreneurship and Urban Growth: An Empirical Assessment with Historical Mines". *NBER Working Paper Series.* National Bureau of Economic Research.

point.[24] As one city's inclusion in this book and the other's absence can attest to, Chinitz's theory has stood the test of time. Whether a city like Pittsburgh's core industrial history is the prevailing reason for its seemingly low level of entrepreneurship in the decades that followed manufacturing decline or not, it is clear that boosting this entrepreneurial output in a city that has been lacking will have inversely proportionate positive economic outcomes.

In 2013, researchers set out to quantify and map out the entrepreneurial spirit across regions of the U.S., Germany, and the United Kingdom. It uses such measures as the Kauffman index of entrepreneurial activity, establishment (new location for an existing firm), entry rate, and business foundation rate, among others to rank different states and regions by their entrepreneurial spirit.

The Rust Belt and Heartland regions, as well as the specific states where our comeback cities are found ranked particularly low in entrepreneurial spirit, described as "an old industrial region that in the past may have attracted (and selected) nonentrepreneurial workers for rule-driven mass production

24 Chinitz, Benjamin. 1961. "Contrasts in Agglomeration: New York and Pittsburgh." *The American Economic Review.* 51, no. 2: 279-89. http://www.jstor.org/stable/1914493.

and socialized their residents through this type of work and related values and norms."[25]

Similar to the Chinitz hypothesis.

Because of the roles generations past played in major manufacturing operations, there was no need for them to flex their entrepreneurial muscles, so to speak. The massive corporations took care of workers and provided stability and benefits, while these corporations took care of much of the larger regional and economic development. This social contract worked great while manufacturing persisted, but once the employers left, the entrepreneurial rust that laid dormant within these cities' inhabitants needed to be shaken off (pun intended—I promise there will be no more rust puns throughout this book, but I had to get that out of my system).

For many years, it remained dormant. However, these cities are beginning to show their true entrepreneurial colors in the hope that, like Silicon Valley rode a wave of ideas and creators to its prominence, so too can the comeback cities.

---

25 Obschonka, M., Schmitt-Rodermund, E., Silbereisen, R. K., Gosling, S. D., & Potter, J. 2013. "The regional distribution and correlates of an entrepreneurship-prone personality profile in the United States, Germany, and the United Kingdom: A socioecological perspective". *Journal of Personality and Social Psychology.*

After all, "The world would be much better if we had 50 more Silicon Valleys," according to Marc Andreessen, co-founder and general partner of Andreessen Horowitz.[26] But more on that theory later.

The bottom line is: these cities have gotten where they are with low or no levels of entrepreneurship. Just imagine the possibilities if that spirit takes flight.

* * *

Is there a link between a city's level of entrepreneurship and economic indicators such as employment and income?

Statistically? Maybe.

Logically? Yes.

According to a study on the regional impact of entrepreneurship:

> *The most entrepreneurial regions in the nation experience greater growth in employment, wages, and productivity*

---

26 Gallagher, Billy. 2013. "Marc Andreessen: The World Would Be Much Better If We Had 50 More Silicon Valleys". *Techcrunch*. https://techcrunch.com/2013/04/20/marc-andreessen-the-world-would-be-much-better-if-we-had-50-more-silicon-valleys/.

when compared with the least entrepreneurial regions. Moreover, that research noted that since innovation may be portable, by itself it is not sufficient for economic growth. [Entrepreneurship] culture is place-based and can be influenced by local and regional policies. In other words, entrepreneurship enhances the regional economic impact of investments in innovations, and commercializing activities undertaken by local entrepreneurs are necessary to convert a region's innovation assets to long-term economic gain. This suggests that interventions aimed at increasing entrepreneurial activities, especially in regions where the birth rate of new start-ups is low, could contribute to increased economic growth.[27]

That is a lengthy way of saying that even with people innovating in a city, there needs to be a culture that supports entrepreneurship to turn these innovative ideas into things that can create actual economic growth.

Although, still far from what many would consider a return to prominence, St. Louis, Missouri has evolved in a major way over the past decade. Once known for its massive companies (Anheuser-Busch, Nestlé Purina Petcare, A.G. Edwards, McDonnell Douglas) and economic conservatism, the city

---

27 Austrian, Ziona & Piazza, Merissa. 2014. "Barriers and Opportunities for Entrepreneurship in Older Industrial Regions". 215-243.

faced a new reality when each of these former stalwart companies left town or closed in the 1990s and early 2000s.[28]

Compared to the nation as a whole, which has seen a steady decline in the percentage of annual new businesses (more than twelve percent founded in the past year in 1980 compared to just eight percent founded in the past year in 2014), St. Louis has managed to increase its percentage of new companies over the past five years, from approximately six percent to well over the national average at nearly ten percent in 2014.[29]

There are admittedly drawbacks in this data such as the inability to tease out startups and small businesses separately, but the trend is supported by local perception of the amount of entrepreneurial activity in the city as of late.

St. Louis serial entrepreneur Keith Alper believes there is considerable potential for St. Louis in both financial technology (fintech) and life sciences. On the fintech front, companies such as Edward Jones and Wells Fargo advisors are headquartered locally, while Mastercard maintains their

---

28 Casselman, Ben. 2019. "Cities Hunt for Startup Magic". *WSJ*.
    https://www.wsj.com/articles/SB10001424127887324904004578539
    373656398096.
29 Casselman, Ben. 2016. "St. Louis is the New Startup Frontier". *Fivethirtyeight*. https://fivethirtyeight.com/features/
    st-louis-is-the-new-startup-frontier/.

global operations center in St. Louis. Monsanto, a long-time agrochemical company, has the foundation to breed other successes around life sciences.

Washington University of St. Louis.

St. Louis University.

Favorable regulatory and tax environment versus the coasts.

Quality of life.

Centrally located and accessible by rail, river, air, and freight.

Affordable cost of labor.

These traits are easy to point out as reasons St. Louis can be a great place to start up a company, but these same traits can be said about many cities.

So, what's made the difference for St. Louis in the past decade?

Many locals point to T-REX incubator, home to more than 200 startup companies, that has created more than 4,000 jobs in St. Louis since 2011 and is responsible for more than $600 million of economic output. Through its facilities, programming, and entrepreneur support services, T-REX seeks to increase the vitality of the regional economy. This nonprofit incubator is described by its executive director Patty Hagen, "This isn't work we're doing, but we're the context for it, we're where this is happening. This is what's accomplished by our partners and young companies coming together in a space like this."[30]

Clearly, it's not just about volume of companies created or pumping money into potential entrepreneurs. More than anything, it is about building an entrepreneurial culture. A physical place along with a mind-set that can spark opportunity and collaboration.

Having created this entrepreneurial culture, it is no wonder St. Louis has seen above average rates of new company generation. Over the same time period of increased firm generation, a study of older industrial cities by the Brookings Institution considers St. Louis to be one of the stronger cities of this variety, noting that income and employment are increasing at faster rates than peer cities.

* * *

---

30 Faulk, Mike. 2017. "T-Rex Touts Thousands of Jobs, Millions of Dollars in Economic Output". *St. Louis Dispatch.* 2017. https://www.stltoday.com/business/local/t-rex-touts-thousands-of-jobs-millions-of-dollars-in/article_bd38bb9e-6672-53d7-b1e0-e319b587072e.html.

Let's boil it down:

- Startups = job creation. But more specifically, rooted job creation that can anchor a community.
- These places are relatively untapped in terms of entrepreneurial potential. Tapping this will reap huge benefits.
- There is evidence that more "entrepreneurial" cities have better overall economic and well-being indicators than cities that are less so.

Finally, nobody is going to save them from the outside. For comeback cities, sustained resurgence must be built from within.

CHAPTER 4

WHAT THIS BOOK
IS AND IS NOT

———

What the following chapters examine is a number of themes that came up over my dive into interviews and research about comeback cities, along with months spent working with Techstars on the ground to develop Buffalo's entrepreneurial ecosystem.

What it is not is a comprehensive assessment of each of the comeback city's entrepreneurial ecosystem.

Instead, what I've done is identify a number of traits—both structural and cultural—that continued to arise across research into all seven comeback cities. Structural traits are those that relate to the resource components of an entrepreneurial ecosystem (e.g., funding and talent). Cultural traits are those that are ingrained into the community's fabric and help make these cities uniquely ripe to ride a wave of entre-preneurship to economic resurgence.

Structural Traits
Differentiators to build on
Just the right size
Dollars go further
Industry integration
Abundance of brains
Big companies = big help
Cultural Traits
Love of place
Collegiality and connection
Fatalism, realism, and optimism
No fake it 'til you make it
Eager for a winning culture
Limited options then, unlimited potential now

In discussing each trait, I will use stories and examples from comeback cities to illustrate the points. While my personal experience in Buffalo results in a heavy dose of narrative from the Nickel City, I aim to use stories from whichever come-back cities most exemplify each particular trait. Regardless of the examples used, each of the traits identified is largely ubiquitous across comeback cities and are part of the overall rationale for recognizing the potential that this group has to reach an entrepreneurship-driven renaissance.

Alongside geographic scope constraints, I also chose not to delve into a number of challenges and needs facing virtually all cities outside of the primary markets (Silicon Valley, New York, Boston, Seattle, Austin, Denver, etc.) as I did not consider them to be unique to comeback cities. The two most commonly mentioned issues facing secondary markets at large are:

- Historical, social, and political challenges
- Capital deficiencies

I want to acknowledge their importance and recognize these barriers to progress. It would be disingenuous to completely disregard these ongoing challenges, and each one deserves (and in many cases already has) its own dedicated historians, researchers, advocates, and libraries of literature.

* * *

Historical, Social, and Political Challenges

"I love Buffalo. I'd like to remain involved and build things there. But it will have to be from afar. For as long as I can remember, I knew I didn't want to *live* there. It just felt too segregated - by race and class - when I knew there were places less so that I could live."

As described by a Buffalo native now living in a major metropolitan area, each city has its own historical, social, and political traits that prevent it from reaching its maximum capacity as an entrepreneurial hub. The prevailing barrier to reaching capacity is a lack of inclusivity, regardless of the city. The root causes, complexities, and manifestations of unequal access to opportunity and involvement—particularly in a space like entrepreneurship and startups, which requires certain knowledge, connections, credibility, and in many cases capital—are massive and pervasive.

Racial and socioeconomic exclusion of groups and individuals from the startup community, oftentimes cemented in invisible geographic boundaries that divide neighborhoods within cities, is an obstacle that must be overcome for any ecosystem to achieve its potential. To pretend otherwise would be utterly ignorant. Being cognizant of this exclusion that has been very much in-your-face for decades and centuries is a must, and the more people who let the community-first mind-set necessary for any good startup ecosystem deep into their bones, the closer we will be to reaching that potential.

While I will generally hold further discussion of these inequalities and exclusivity for experts able to give them their due examination, one example that is pertinent to one of the comeback cities is worth sharing to show the numerous and often unperceived ways that these issues impact entrepreneurial development.

According to a Manhattan Institute study examining racial separation in large American cities, although segregation has declined to some degree across the board in the past century, St. Louis remains one of the most segregated cities in the country. This determination was made based on dissimilarity and isolation indexes, which look at the extent that racial groups tend to live in equal proportion in city neighborhoods and the extent to which neighborhoods have vastly different racial makeups, respectively.[31]

But you don't need a study to tell you this. Anyone who has lived in St. Louis can tell you the same.

One prominent example of this separation is known as the "Delmar Divide," a difference in economic and racial makeup on opposite sides of Delmar Boulevard. At its most extreme along the nearly ten miles of divide, opposite neighborhoods

---

31   Glaeser, Edward, and Jacob Vigdor. 2012. "The End of the Segregated Century: Racial Separation in America's Neighborhoods, 1890–2010". *Manhattan Institute CSLL Civic Report*, no. 66.

across Delmar Boulevard see home prices to the north average $78,000 while they go for an average of $310,000 just south. Average income to the north ($22,000) is less than half of what it is to the south ($47,000). North of Delmar in the neighborhoods of Lewis Place and Fountain Park, the population is ninety-nine percent black and five percent hold a bachelor's degree, while the southern neighboring portion of Central West End is seventy percent white and sixty-seven percent hold a bachelor's degree.[32]

Another major source of inequality in St. Louis comes from when it split into St. Louis City and St. Louis County in 1876. The region has considered options to reunite the two on multiple occasions, including an ongoing proposition in present day. The original split happened before the city grew and sprawled, and was driven by city residents not wanting to pay taxes for the ~27,000 county residents.

A St. Louis magazine article from 2014 on dividing lines in St. Louis describes the effects:

> *Urban geographers describe St. Louis as a donut hole—*
> *empty in the middle and encircled by doughy counties.*
> *Cities like Denver, Seattle, and Portland, Oregon, would*
> *be custard-filled, with appealing city centers and no gaps*

---

32   Bartley, Joshua. 2017. "Breaking Down the Delmar Divide". *Next-stl*. https://nextstl.com/2017/09/breaking-delmar-divide/.

in the urban landscape. Here, white flight was followed by middle-class black flight, and historically black communities in the city were razed for the sake of "urban renewal," highway construction, and tax-increment-financing redevelopment projects.[33]

Just in this one city, its historic position and transition through the racial, political, industrial, and other economic events of the twentieth century have undoubtedly impacted the way that it must now move forward. Each city has its own variations of unequal opportunity and participation in entrepreneurial development. There is no doubt that continuing to encourage, support, fund, and generally include individuals from all circles will unleash potential within entrepreneurial communities in cities and regions across the country.

"Continuing to encourage" even still feels too shallow. For a firsthand account for what some of this historic divide feels like, I highly recommend reading Marsha Music's piece in the anthology *Voices from the Rust Belt* titled "The Kidnapped Children of Detroit", which gives a young girl's perspective on the white flight that occurred in Detroit in the second half of the twentieth century.

---

33 Cooperman, Jeannette. 2014. "The Story Of Segregation In St. Louis". *Stlmag.* https://www.stlmag.com/news/the-color-line-race-in-st.-louis/.

* * *

Capital Deficiencies

The first structural hinderance to substantial startup growth in secondary markets (think everywhere from Portland, OR to Portland ME, inclusive of all comeback cities and others outside of primary markets mentioned above) that will often come up is the lack of capital. Years ago, it was venture capital as a whole, with particular focus now on lack of early stage funding to get startups through their initial phase of getting off the ground.

Quick lesson for those not here from a startup background: Early stage funding typically includes the first couple of rounds of the venture capital funding process (money from investment groups who focus on startup investing, referred to as venture capitalists). You'll hear Series A and Series B typically included in this category of early stage funding, and, depending on who you ask, they could also include seed funding from angel investors (individually wealthy investors). Seed stage funding typically is provided to companies less than two years of age, while Series A and Series B funding rounds occur later in the company's development and consists of larger investment amounts.[34]

---

34 Wagner, Allen. "The Venture Capital Lifecycle". 2014. *Pitchbook*. https://pitchbook.com/news/articles/the-venture-capital-lifecycle.

By no means has the amount of early stage funding caught up to that of the major markets (case in point: the primary data element for Revolution's Rise of the Rest Seed fund, an investment fund seeking to remedy this flaw, is that seventy-five percent of all venture capital goes to New York, California, and Massachusetts), but those who are intimately involved in this world will increasingly tell you that it is actually the lack of growth stage funding that prevents secondary entrepreneurial cities from really ramping up. These rounds of funding typically involve venture capital firms and are greater than $2 million. These investments allow companies to scale up dramatically in terms of customer acquisition, production, and delivery. Think about it like a company that has grown from idea to product and now needs a large influx of cash to increase production of that product at a much larger scale.

When considering the impact of a startup on a city, it is this growth stage where job creation really becomes tangible for the larger community. The more growth stage funding that becomes available to secondary markets, the greater the economic impact these companies will have on the city and regional economy.

At the same time, founders and ecosystem supporters in many "Tier-2" cities like the comeback cities will say that what is holding back their particular community is not seed stage or growth stage funding, but stages even before that. It is the $5,000 and $10,000 bets from colleagues and your rich aunt and uncle that is required to keep early companies afloat. There is not enough people like that in secondary markets.

As you can tell, there are capital constraints at every level. The bottom line is that funding will always be a challenge at some stage depending on your company, industry, team, market, and a plethora of other factors. It is important to acknowledge this, but for the sake of trying to focus on shared traits across this grouping of cities, much of those ins and outs will be excluded from the research presented in this book.

* * *

Because the topics outlined here affect virtually all secondary startup markets, they will not be examined through the lens of comeback cities throughout the remainder of this book. Instead, we will focus on the unique aspects of these seven cities that influence their current and future abilities to promote entrepreneurship as a vehicle to greater community prosperity.

CHAPTER 5

DON'T BE MAD YOUR CITY DIDN'T MAKE THE CUT

──────

While the geographic scope of this book is constrained to just those seven cities defined as comeback cities, I have to give due respect to the many other cities that share some of the traits discussed in this book. From my wanderings, my attention has been called to countless other suggested cities, all of which share much of the pride and potential as those cities included in this book. If you find this topic interesting, I urge you to look more into these cities and the many books exploring their past, present, and future.

In taking on this endeavor, one of the first things I realized was that I needed to put some parameters on the grouping of cities I researched. As a result, some cities are going to inevitably be left out. But that's no reason to take offense—in many cases, your city likely didn't make it as a comeback city because it had not fallen into as deep of an economic downturn as those that ultimately were included. That being said, there are countless cities that share some of the traits of comeback cities and do warrant some limelight for their efforts around growing through startups and entrepreneurship.

So, friends from Indianapolis, I hear you. Columbus natives, don't yell at me.

Relatives in Chattanooga, former classmates and colleagues from Newark, and friends everywhere else, without further ado I'd like to give you your due shine.

Indianapolis, for starters, you didn't come close to the cutoff of having lost more than one-third peak population. In fact, there has only been one decade in recent history that your population decreased and it was a single-digit drop-off. One of the remarkable aspects of Indianapolis's recent economy has been the contributions of successful entrepreneur Scott Dorsey into the entrepreneurial ecosystem. Referred to in prior and future chapters as a success story, ExactTarget was founded by Dorsey, Chris Baggott, and Peter McCormick in 2000 and sold to Salesforce for $2.5 billion thirteen years later. Just two years after that, Dorsey co-founded venture studio High Alpha in Indianapolis which has now become one of the premier pieces driving Indianapolis to become "one of the most promising tech ecosystems globally."[35]

Columbus, you didn't even come close to the historic decline necessary to make the cut either. In fact, your city's population has continued to climb decade after decade for more than a century. Beyond that criterial exclusion, you have already become a dominant Midwest startup city. With multiple major West Coast investors moving to Columbus to provide much needed venture capital support, the city saw a $1 billion-plus acquisition of Columbus-based Cover-MyMeds by San Francisco's McKesson in 2017 and has seen considerable growth in the number of high-caliber, high-growth startups in the past decade. In the 2017 edition of the annual Kauffman Foundation growth entrepreneurship index, Columbus was the third ranked city in the country in growth entrepreneurship activity, behind only Washington, DC and Austin, TX.[36]

All in all, Columbus, you might just be too *cool* for the likes of this book.

---

35 "High Alpha Raises Over $100M to Launch High Alpha Studio II and High Alpha Capital II". 2018. *High Alpha.* https://highalpha. com/introducing-high-alpha-ii/.

36 Morelix, Arnobio, and Josh Russell-Fritch. 2017. "Kauffman Index of Growth Entrepreneurship". *Kauffman Foundation.* https://www.kauffman.org/kauffman-index/reporting/-/media/ e37f4200462347dbb0d385e01e656be2.ashx.

Nashville, rolling in just one spot behind Columbus in the growth entrepreneurship activity rankings, has seen a similar rise in recent memory. Not only was Music City the only U.S. location in the top ten of National Geographic's recent rankings of the "coolest" destinations on the planet for its cultural prowess, but it has seen startup success stories such as Emma, Jumpstart, and AmpliFly Entertainment propel it forward as a startup destination as well.[37,38] As for the criteria of comeback cities, Nashville did not see the same kind of deindustrialization to group it with the comeback cities. The city has remained between twentieth and twenty-fifth in U.S. population rankings for the past four decades. With their entrepreneurial-based growth, though, I fully anticipate they will crack the top twenty very soon.

Newark, you were in the running as a comeback city for certain, based on population trends, as you lost nearly forty-four percent of your population from 1930 to 2000, but because of recent growth in 2010 the timeline of decline and comeback didn't align with the rest of the group. Upon further digging, some of the decline was due to the success and sprawl of pharmaceutical companies to areas outside of Newark's city limits. Because the economic downturn did not

37 "The Cool List 2018". 2019. *National Geographic.* https://www.nationalgeographic.co.uk/travel/2017/12/cool-list-2018.

38 "Why It's a Great Time to be a Tech Startup in Nashville". 2018. *Growthwright.* https://growthwright.com/blog/great-time-to-be-tech-startup-in-nashville/.

follow the same industrial shocks and timeline, Newark was not economically or socially aligned as much as the chosen comeback cities. On the bright side, recent growth and recognition for Newark as a potential pharmaceutical startup hotbed leave me optimistic that the city is well on its way to its own version of a comeback.

Kansas City, I'd like to think of you as our comeback cities' kindred, but more diversified sibling. You share many cultural traits with our comeback cities, and lost some national prominence due to deindustrialization, but did not see the steep decline that comeback cities saw. If I were to pinpoint the driving factor for this different shock response, it was that comeback cities were hyper-specialized while Kansas City was not. Instead of putting all of its eggs in one or two major industry baskets and going wayward when that industry did, Kansas City was diversified enough to withstand. That being said, only recently has Kansas City really turned a corner in terms of entrepreneurship-driven economic redevelopment. Since the early 2010s, Kansas City has become a sterling example of what can be accomplished in this arena in only a decade. The turnaround began in 2011 when Google Fiber announced Kansas City as their pilot city, allowing the city to see that if a tech brand like that believed in it, residents should too. With this catalyst, the city began to see the pieces for a thriving startup ecosystem appear—from capital to support resources to density of startup activity facilitated by city infrastructure.

Now, instead of simply being a kindred spirit of comeback cities, Kansas City can be an example.

New Orleans, you represent a truly high culture, relatively low-cost city for entrepreneurs to kick off their gig. To be honest, this city met the criteria of a comeback city: historic size and relevance alongside a significant drop-off in peak population by more than one-third. Given the unique circumstances of the decline associated with Hurricane Katrina, though, the historic economic timetable didn't align with the other comeback cities enough to include New Orleans in the group. I liken the economic decline of comeback cities associated with deindustrialization to that of cancer or heart disease, in comparison to the heart attack-like downturn that New Orleans experienced as a result of Hurricane Katrina. The impacts of both types of shock are crushing and far-reaching, but the effects and recovery efforts are too dissimilar to readily explore common themes. Similar to many of our other not-quite-comeback cities, though, New Orleans has—in many ways—even more going for it in terms of startup-driven economic revival than the comeback cities themselves.

Milwaukee, you may be the closest nonfit of all the cities not included as a comeback city. This city had a similar manufacturing past, including a drop-off in the 1970s and beyond, but lost only about twenty percent of its peak population as a result of deindustrialization. A number of factors including slightly more industry diversification than the comeback cities resulted in Milwaukee's parallel, but less drastic timeline. Today, Milwaukee is seeing signs of rebirth including a construction boom, with more than $5 billion recently put into a multitude of construction projects focusing in hospitality and tourist attractions.[39] From a startup perspective, a 2018 Surge Cities Index created by Inc. magazine and Startup Genome, Milwaukee was ranked twenty-ninth out of fifty cities based on an index combining more than a half-dozen factors. Within those factors, Milwaukee ranked third for net business creation and eighth for job growth, showing signs that the surge has already begun.[40]

Chattanooga, you've also been popping up as a sneaky "cool" spot. The conversation usually goes something like:

"Hey, you know where else you should look?"

39 Dienst, Jennifer. "Former Rust Belt Cities Rise Again as Innovation Hubs". 2019. *PCMA*. https://www.pcma.org/rust-belt-cities-reinvent-innovation-hubs-knowledge-economies/.

40 Schuyler, David, and Bill Cieslewicz. 2018. "Milwaukee Ranks Among Best Cities to Start a Business". *Milwaukee Business Journal*. https://www.bizjournals.com/milwaukee/news/2018/12/26/milwaukee-ranks-among-best-cities-to-start-a.html.

"Columbus?"

"No."

"Indianapolis?"

"Nope."

"Chattanooga?"

"YES. How'd you know?"

To be honest, it had originally come up because of my relatives that live there (shoutout to the Clifford family). But from a startup perspective, people have been raving about it as a hidden gem. It has become a growing hotspot for transportation logistics, with FedEx being a feeder of talent because transportation logistics is a legacy industry there. It is being called "freight alley" and "the Silicon Valley of trucking," and estimates indicate that the Chattanooga area has approximately 7,000 white-collar professionals involved in freight logistics, not including drivers or warehouse workers.[41] Cool? I'd say so.

---

41   Pare, Mike. "Moving Fast: The Freight Services Sector is Riding High in Chattanooga, 'The Silicon Valley Of Trucking'". 2019. *Chattanooga Times Free Press.* https://www.timesfreepress.com/news/edge/story/2019/oct/01/moving-fast-freight-services-sector-riding-hi/504428/.

One of the tenants of a strong entrepreneurial community is one that acts with an abundance mind-set rather than a scarcity mind-set. In that spirit, I am happy to report that each of these cities that didn't quite make the cut as a comeback city have their own reasons to be optimistic. There is, after all, plenty of startup success to go around.

PART 2

STRUCTURAL TRAITS: INDUSTRY, INSTITUTIONS, AND EXPERTISE

"It is the frontier of innovation, and it really is the opportunity of a lifetime to see this next economy swelling."

—CHRIS OLSEN

* * *

When I first took an accounting class and learned about tangible assets compared to intangible assets, it was just about the first thing that clicked instantly in that course for me. Tangible assets: I can touch (buildings, inventory, etc.). Intangible assets: I can't touch (brand recognition or intellectual property). Now, just as I was about to begin considering myself as an honorary Certified Public Accountant (CPA) in that moment, the professor brings about the idea of goodwill and my mental train went back off the track. Don't worry if you don't know about what goodwill is in the accounting world yet. We'll cover that in the next part.

In this book, we will talk about structural and cultural traits of this group of comeback cities. Think of the former as tangible assets and the latter as intangible assets. Again, I'll save my attempt at explaining goodwill for later on, but for now let's talk about these cities' structural traits. These are the traits that investors can point to as an advantage that a company in a comeback city would have in a certain area compared to a city elsewhere. We'll span the topics of industries, institutions, and expertise that have developed in these cities.

Structural traits identified as common traits across comeback cities include:

1. Differentiators to build on—each city has its own value proposition from past prominence upon which to grow.
2. Just the right size—comeback cities are big enough to matter on a bigger scale, but small enough to act on a shared vision.

3. Dollars go further—whether you're a founder, investor, or everyday citizen, you get more bang for your buck.

4. Industry integration—key industries for our nation's future prosperity exist as strengths in comeback cities.

5. Abundance of brains—universities and generations of industry expertise exist, giving these cities a strong potential talent pipeline.

6. Big companies = big help—comeback cities are home to countless large, long-standing corporations that are a difference maker in helping create a strong startup community.

CHAPTER 6

DIFFERENTIATORS
TO BUILD ON

———

"One of the great lies of life is to follow your passion...don't follow your passion."

This simple statement, perhaps Mark Cuban's most widely cited pieces of advice for entrepreneurs, is sure to rile up many entrepreneurs. While there is some merit in the statement alone, Cuban goes on to explain himself, "The things I ended up being really good at were the things I found myself putting effort into. A lot of people talk about passion, but that's really not what you need to focus on...The things I ended up being really good at were the things I found myself putting effort into."[42]

---

42 Clifford, Catherine. 2018. "Billionaire Mark Cuban: 'One of the Great Lies of Life is Follow Your Passions'". *CNBC*. https://www. cnbc.com/2018/02/16/mark-cuban-follow-your-passion-is-bad-advice.html.

If you are reading this book, you are likely familiar with Mark Cuban. But if you are not, the long and short of it is that Mark grew up in one of the comeback cities, Pittsburgh, PA, without any familial wealth or inherent advantage as an entrepreneur. He is now one of the most popular names in sports and investing, and is likely one of the first names the general public thinks of when they hear the word "mogul."

* * *

We're talking about cities, after all, so finding the "passion" of an entire metropolitan area doesn't make a ton of sense. Sure, each city has its own spirit and characteristics, but boiling an entire population down to a limited number of things they are passionate about is unrealistic.

Instead, it is Cuban's explanation of chasing those things that you find yourself putting effort into that comeback cities can and should apply to their own redevelopment. This includes both the dominant industries of the past and those new areas that have the greatest momentum based on recent development, founder success, and resources. What are the differentiators each of these cities has that it can build on and pivot from for the future?

It's easy to look at Detroit, called Motor City because of its historic dominance in the automotive industry, and say *that* is what makes Detroit tick. *That* is Detroit's "passion" that it should chase if it wants to be great again.

Kind of.

Because of its standing as Motor City, Detroit has a number of resources that it would be wise to make use of, including car giants like Ford and a population with generations of know-how. But the car industry is not what it used to be and for a number of complex reasons, Detroit will never own that industry again.

In recognition of this fact, Detroit has hustled to reinvent itself as a hub of mobility and the future of transportation. At the same time, to focus an entire city's efforts around one industry would be to repeat the mistakes of the past that led to much of the city's recent economic woes. This is where Cuban's advice to focus on not what you are passionate about, but what you find yourself putting the most effort into comes into play.

A startup-driven economic revival must be led by company founders. It cannot be dictated from any state or local government, or outside pundits. Companies that find traction and success will dictate the future focus of the city. If it is done well, there will be a number of focuses and successful industries.

If comeback cities can reinvent themselves to make use of their past expertise while diversifying their portfolio by supporting successful founders across other industries, this is a recipe for a renaissance.

* * *

A company's value proposition is not only what value it provides to its customers, but also what sets it apart from other competitors in the market. A brand may stand out for its quality products (e.g., Steinway grand pianos, Pyrex glassware), its customer service (e.g., Trader Joe's, Zappos), or its value per dollar (e.g., Ikea, Honda). In most cases, it is this differentiator that drives a company's success. In some rare cases such as modern tech giants Google and Amazon, companies are able to excel in multiple arenas with multiple value propositions.

If we look at modern American cities based on their economic and industry differentiators, such as New York, San Francisco, Boston, Seattle, and a select few others, they may be able to mirror the tech giants in excelling across arenas. They have the startup resources—talent, funding, entrepreneurial support, and educational institutions—to build their startup scene across a multitude of industries (finance, medicine, pharmaceuticals, advanced manufacturing, etc.).

Comeback cities, on the other hand, are typically those with a strong foundation in once-booming manufacturing industries that are no more. Without a head start in many areas the business world is clamoring for, the likelihood of growing these cities and burgeoning a true, sustainable comeback on the shoulders of the latest technology disruptors is low. Instead, like the Trader Joe's and Ikeas of the world, these cities must find a way to differentiate to attract the initial interest and gain the initial momentum to expand into new niches and achieve that comeback.

According to the Brookings Institution, "In a knowledge economy it's about what your people know and how to do it. It's not what your machines are good at. [Each of the former industrial cities has] talent, it's got vestiges of its industrial past that are actually finding new forms of value in the modern economy."[43]

Pittsburgh Mayor Bill Peduto has made the comparison of Carnegie Mellon, along with the University of Pittsburgh, to the iron ore factories that made this city an industrial power in the nineteenth century. The schools are the local resource

---

43 Walker, Melody. 2018. "Brookings Report: St. Louis' Economy Doing Better Than Many Older Industrial Cities". *Stl Public Radio.* https://news.stlpublicradio.org/post/brookings-report-st-lou-is-economy-doing-better-many-older-industrial-cities#stream/0.

"churning out that talent" from which the city is fueled.[44] As such, a city like Pittsburgh has reassessed its new natural resources—such as its renowned robotics educational institutions—to pursue a new niche that it is uniquely equipped to thrive in.

* * *

What does it look like in modern comeback cities to take advantage of dominant industries of the past while modernizing for renewed momentum?

Before I answer that directly, let's take a stroll down a cinematic side street for a moment.

It reminds me of one of my favorite comeback stories of all time, that depicted in the movie *Cinderella Man*. A true story about a Great Depression era boxer named James J. Braddock, this film has a lesson to impart to comeback cities. After a dominant record of 44-2-2 in his young career, Braddock climbed the rankings until he earned a heavyweight championship title fight opportunity in 1929. In a fifteen-round

---

44   Carpenter, Mackenzie & Todd, Deborah. "The Google Effect: How Has The Tech Giant Changed Pittsburgh's Commerce And Culture?". 2019. *Pittsburgh Post-Gazette.* https://www.post-gazette.com/business/tech-news/2014/12/07/Google-effect-How-has-tech-giant-changed-Pittsburgh-s-commerce-and-culture/stories/201412040291.

decision, Braddock lost the fight and broke his dominant hand in the process, beginning a sharp decline of fortunes. After steadily becoming obsolete in the boxing world, he spent nearly a year grinding to make ends meet and trying to find regular work on the docks. Not exactly what he envisioned at the height of his boxing career. For many of the comeback cities, this rock bottom period occurred at the end of the twentieth century, when the population was largely out of work and had to seek opportunities elsewhere.

If you have not seen the movie, I'm sure you can imagine what happened next based on the title. After being given an unlikely chance in a big fight once again, Braddock shocked the world and ended up with an unimaginable run of victories. Part of Braddock's revival was a result of an unintentional reinvention of his fighting style. After originally breaking his right hand, he had to learn how to fight in an unconventional way that favored what was previously a weakness, his nondominant hand. The injuries to his right hand, what was once a disadvantage, gave his skill set a new dimension that propelled his ascent from the deepest pit of his life all the way to heavyweight champion of the world.

Although none of the comeback cities have come close to the level of a world champion like Braddock, each is in varying stages of regeneration. Regardless of what stage each city is in, there is a lesson to be learned from the reinvention of

Braddock's fighting style. Whether it is finding a new way to make the most of past industrial dominance like Detroit, or finding a new niche entirely like Cleveland seems to be doing, being able to pivot strategically to be positioned for the needs of tomorrow will be key to these cities' return to prominence.

* * *

Let's look closer at Cleveland's story. Cleveland has a number of strong educational institutions, led by Case Western Reserve University, capable of providing strong technology and engineering talent. There is no particular reason it would be unable to make waves in a burgeoning technology like blockchain if the city collectively put its resources towards becoming a hub; however, momentum and existing efforts are not on its side.

Cities such as New York and San Francisco have grown into epicenters for blockchain technology as a whole. Instead of reallocating its collective efforts to unseat the existing blockchain hubs, Cleveland could seek to do what Cleveland already does better than anywhere else. Cleveland could seek to do what Cleveland has more resources to do than anywhere else.

Because Cleveland is among the top cities for the health and medical industries, riding the existing momentum of this wave is what is going to carry the city's redevelopment furthest. Not to dismiss the potential of technologies like blockchain, but one avenue for Cleveland to take advantage of their current position would be to focus on the application of such technologies to their already advantageous industries. Cleveland HeartLab, for instance, specializes in tests that evaluate cardiovascular disease risk, and was acquired by Quest Diagnostics. This kind of company is the kind of success story that we can hope to see more out of Cleveland in the future.

Even cities like Detroit, for which its forte and livelihood seem to have turned to ash, can utilize past efforts and resources to revive and reinvent industries of yesteryear. Technologies coming from Detroit, with the benefit of nearby University of Michigan in Ann Arbor, include autonomous vehicles and the associated sensing technology. As mentioned previously, this has positioned the former manufacturing behemoth as the future hub of mobility in the U.S.

A good example to point to in Detroit is the North American International Auto Show (NAIAS). NAIAS (then the Detroit Auto Show) debuted at the turn of the twentieth century and would annually display new car debuts from American and International (beginning in 1957) automakers.[45] Today, the

45 Moutzalias, Tanya. "Early 1900s Photos Show the Early Years of the Detroit Auto Show". 2018. *Mlive.* https://www.mlive.com/

scope of the show has expanded to include a concurrent event called AutoMobil-D to exhibit mobility technology.[46] Detroit itself had more mobility startup exhibitors at NAIAS in 2017 than any other city in the world.

Many national experts in building entrepreneurial ecosystems would argue that capitalizing on past success is a secondary strategy. Future niches should instead be based on what industries the community's founders are investing their energy in. However, I think these strategies go hand in hand. In many cases, such as those described above in Pittsburgh, Cleveland, and Detroit, founders are led to industries in which their locale has an abundance of talent and resources. While this is not the only route to finding your city's niche, it can be the most advantageous for comeback cities.

news/detroit/2018/01/historic_photos_of_the_detroit.html.

46 Saunders, Pete. "Detroit: America's Newest Tech Hub". 2019. *Forbes*. https://www.forbes.com/sites/petesaunders1/2017/02/15/detroit-americas-newest-tech-hub/#c899d129faf1.

CHAPTER 7

JUST THE RIGHT SIZE

———

When I first tried to figure out where to begin gaining an understanding of the startup scene in Buffalo, I was surprised at how easily I was put in touch with all the right people. I imagined how long it would take me to feel like I had even a remote handle on the scope of the scene if I had tried to do the same thing in San Francisco.

Although there are hundreds of individuals in dozens of roles that make up the Buffalo startup ecosystem (as is the case in any city), I was put in touch with a dozen or so individuals who seemed to be at the epicenter of efforts to grow that ecosystem.

One of which is 43North, an investment group that runs a state-funded annual startup pitch competition in which $5 million is awarded, but also operates a hub of innovation in the form of a coworking space for all of its portfolio companies in downtown Buffalo and works across the relatively small startup community to integrate and collaborate as much as possible. Based on this understanding of 43North's role, I was not surprised to hear from President and Chief Executive Officer (CEO) Alex Gress that the most promising aspect of Buffalo's entrepreneurial ecosystem is its perfect size.

"Big enough to have legitimacy, but small enough to lock arms."

The legitimacy comes from both its past prominence and enduring positive traits such as its people, culture, and architecture. When he refers to locking arms, he is talking about the relatively small entrepreneurial community being able to join together, both physically and ideologically, to unite and form a cohesive, long-term vision for entrepreneurship in Buffalo.

The physical locking of arms is possible for many comeback cities because of their relatively small communities, allowing for the true makers and innovators to create a physical density of entrepreneurship. The strategy of clustering small businesses and startups, especially those that have ties to one another's industries, has been proven to increase innovation and productivity.[47]

One of the most important aspects of being a small enough city to coordinate the entrepreneurial ecosystem development together is the chance to create physical density. Those who study the development of these ecosystems point to density as a key driver of progress, but an element that is often difficult to achieve based on physical limitations within the city or region.

For comeback cities, however, this can be within reach.

Cleveland recently underwent a Techstars assessment of its entrepreneurial ecosystem, and it was determined that there was much to be done to improve the city's density; at the same time, making these improvements for a city like Cleveland is not outside the realm of possibilities.

Cleveland's entrepreneurial activity was found to be segmented across three main locations—LaunchHouse, Flashstarts, and a portion of the network in the city's west end. As such, there are near-term and mid-term actions to be

---

47   McNamer, Bruce & Zeuli, Kim. "Cities Need Small Business Growth Strategies". 2019. *JPMC City Makers*. https://www.theatlantic.com/sponsored/jpmc-city-makers/cities-need-small-business-growth-strategies/149/.

taken to increase the physical density of this network. In the near-term, Techstars recommended that a group of real estate actors meet with a key group of entrepreneurial leaders to determine the optimal location to develop critical mass for the city.

Beyond this, "The city, county and other governmental and quasi-governmental organizations need to develop incentives to recruit as many mid-sized (5-50 people) growth companies as well as all current entrepreneurial organizations to a downtown destination or neighborhood."[48]

The notion that a city with the relevance and potential of Cleveland has the ability to get its key stakeholders in a room with a map to begin to redevelop their entire ecosystem is unique and extremely valuable. Similar conclusions were drawn in an assessment of Buffalo. While there is much to be done to take advantage, the beauty of cities this size is that it is entirely possible.

* * *

Once at the proverbial table, these comeback city players have the unique opportunity to shape a long-term plan for their city, vital for a sustained success across the region. Brad

---

48 "Assessment & Roadmap Report: Cleveland, OH". 2018. *Techstars Startup Community Development Program.*

Feld described the difficulty of aligning timelines across the network of contributors to the ecosystem:

> *Most feeder organizations function differently. Universities function in a one-year time horizon and I like to joke that they have summer off. The government functions in two-to-four-year rhythms with an election year. So they're functioning for one-to-three years, not 20. Big business has a quarterly, annual rhythm. So, you have to be able to transcend all the ups and downs in the shorter-term measurement when you're building the startup community."[49]*

The size and proximity of the players in comeback cities give them the ability to transcend these ups and downs.

Buffalo has taken action to be the model of this united entrepreneurial front. In early 2019, Techstars and 43North partnered on a multi-year program to develop and grow the entrepreneurial ecosystem in the Buffalo-Niagara region. The intent is to build a self-sustaining group of individuals and organizations across all aspects of the ecosystem—from founders to investors to academics to government leaders.

---

49 "Techstars' Brad Feld: A Startup Community Needs a 20-Year Time Horizon". 2013. Podcast. *Knowledge@Wharton*. https://knowledge.wharton.upenn.edu/article/techstars-brad-feld-a-startup-community-needs-a-20-year-time-horizon/.

Full disclosure, I have worked as part of this initiative. But coming from a biased or unbiased perspective, the approach is undoubtedly unique.

According to Vice President of Innovation at Techstars, Chris Heivly:

> Techstars sought a community that had a blend of passion, population size, and the organizational commitment to take their ecosystem and supersize it. Buffalo already has a burgeoning ecosystem with strong players such as 43North, Launch NY, and University at Buffalo. While Techstars is partnering with 43North on this initiative, the Techstars Startup Ecosystem Development program is a community-wide effort, and Techstars will focus on increasing the existing collaboration in the community."[50] Similar efforts are underway in Louisville, KY and a number of international cities including Taipei, Taiwan and Turin, Italy.

The entrepreneur's lifestyle can often be a lonely and isolated one, particularly in the early stages of a company's life cycle. Picture someone working out of their home office, on their

---

50 "Techstars and 43North Partner to Grow Entrepreneurial Ecosystem in Buffalo". 2019. *Techstars Blog.*

https://www.techstars.com/content/accelerators/tech-stars-43north-partner-grow-entrepreneurial-ecosystem-buffalo/.

couch late at night, or out of their garage to get their business off the ground. In places like comeback cities, being an entrepreneur can sometimes still be considered an unorthodox route which can make those who venture down this road feel like an outsider. Without having a group, a cluster, or even a physical place to feel part of a greater entrepreneurial ecosystem, a business's likelihood of success will wane. Moreover, without having success stories around them to see what is possible and how it can be done, entrepreneurs are more likely to fade in their efforts. Take this entrepreneur out of the home office and connect her with a group of other entrepreneurs and big thinkers, and maybe she meets someone whose company now has three to five employees and thinks to herself, "Hey if that person can do it, so can I."

The beauty of comeback cities is they are compact enough for entrepreneurs who want to emerge and grow to know how to be a part of the city's greater vision.

CHAPTER 8

DOLLARS GO FURTHER

———

I haven't seen a lemonade stand in a long time. I'm not sure why that is, and it makes me a little sad. I imagine they're used more often now for half-baked analogies like the one I'm about to make rather than to actually quench anyone's thirst.

Imagine I'm jogging down the road and I see two little kids selling lemonade on either side of the street. Little Nora on your left has a proper farmers market setup going. She's got a big sign that says Nora's Noteworthy Nectars. She has six glass bowls overflowing with fresh lemons on her table. She has her little brother swinging a sign out front like it's a mattress store blowout sale, reading, "$1 per glass."

Across the street I see Abigail's lemonade stand. It's a folding table with nothing on it but a couple rows of those little wax Dixie cups. Flashbacks to rinsing with mouthwash at the dentist fill my head. There is a loose-leaf piece of paper on the table that says "1 cup = 1 quarter." Dental memories aside, that's a good deal.

Now being the cost-conscious, but quality-driven consumer that I am, I take a peek behind both tables before making my decision. Lo and behold, they're both using the same Country Time powdered lemonade mix.

Abigail's stand is a comeback city. Nora's is a thriving startup metropolis like San Francisco. Although I hope all cities can strive toward fresh-squeezed lemonade one day, the lemonade mix is our current entrepreneurial output. Like Nora's lemonade stand, there may be more going on at the surface of the entrepreneurial ecosystem in San Francisco, but you can have access to the same entrepreneurs in a comeback city for a fraction of the cost. Regardless of how each city appears from the outside, entrepreneurs are entrepreneurs no matter where they are.

It's just the support around them—the window dressing, the mentors, the investors—that accounts for the difference in success levels between these entrepreneurs in different geographies.

* * *

Perhaps the most obvious benefit of investing, living, and building a business in comeback cities is that, because of each city's economic size and scope, a dollar goes further than in the booming urban centers elsewhere in the country. The U.S. Department of Commerce's Bureau of Economic Analysis maintains data around Regional Price Parity (RPP) down to the city and county level. RPP is a method of comparing buying power from one metropolitan area to another. The dollar amounts listed for comeback cities below, along with the top metropolitan recipients of recent venture capital, show the real value of $100 in each location.[51,52]

51 VanAntwerp, Tom. "The Real Value of $100 in Metropolitan Areas". 2015. *Tax Foundation*. https://taxfoundation.org/real-value-100-metropolitan-areas-0.

52 Florida, Richard. "High-Tech Startups are Still Concentrated in Just a Few Cities". 2017. *Citylab*. https://www.citylab.com/life/2017/10/venture-capital-concentration/539775/.

Metropolitan Region	Real Value of $100
Cleveland-Elyria, OH	$111.73
St. Louis, MO	$111.48
Cincinnati, OH	$110.50
Buffalo-Cheektowaga-Niagara Falls, NY	$106.61
Pittsburgh, PA	$106.16
Detroit-Warren-Dearborn, MI	$102.56
Baltimore-Columbia-Towson, MD	$91.91
Boston-Cambridge-Newton, MA	$90.17
San Francisco-Oakland-Hayward, CA	$83.13
New York-Newark-Jersey City, NY-NJ	$81.77

Not only do the dollar values in comeback cities mean that
investment dollars (and I mean investment dollars in the
broadest sense—not simply venture capital investments)
can go to fund more talent, resources, branding, research,
manufacturing, and more for each new company, the cost of
living allows potential founders the ability to start something
on the side. Unlike New York City or San Francisco, where
you are more pressed to have a steady, substantial income
stream to pay for housing and other high living expenses, a
place like Buffalo can allow you to subsist as part of the gig

economy while you really try to get your idea or business off the ground.

Housing costs alone set comeback cities apart for founders and new company employees. Median home costs in New York City are nearing $300,000 while they are below $75,000 in Buffalo. In an article about the trend of millennials moving to Buffalo in pursuit of a better, more cost-efficient lifestyle, the Western New York city was compared to its downstate metropolis as such: "If moving to New York City is like dating the most popular kid in your high school only to discover all the blemishes that aren't visible when gazed upon from a distance, then Buffalonians will tell you that moving to their city is like dating the girl next door who's undergoing a She's All That-style transformation."[53]

Like the lemonade stand story from before, I'm not sure this is the perfect analogy, but it helps get us there. Comeback cities have a lot to offer in large part to how much you can squeeze out of a dollar because of the decades-old blemishes that people focus on from afar.

Eric Schmidt, the former chairman of Google's parent company, Alphabet, noted one of the benefits of cities outside

---

53   Teicher, Jordan. "Millennials are Moving to Buffalo & Living Like Kings". 2015. *Gothamist*. https://gothamist.com/news/millennials-are-moving-to-buffalo-living-like-kings.

the primary markets (like comeback cities): "There is a large selection of relatively undervalued businesses in the Heartland between the coasts, some of which can scale quickly."[54]

This simple idea that comparatively, comeback city companies are going to be undervalued and investments are at bargain prices compared to many more traditional venture capital cities is important for investors to realize. Think about the runway that a $600,000 seed round (meaning the amount of time an early stage investment amount allows a company to continue operating for) would give a startup in San Francisco that needed to pay for operating expenses, space rental, and possibly talent. That same runway may be two or three times as long for that company in Cincinnati or Cleveland.

"The investment arbitrage side of this is important. There's not much capital in these places so valuations are lower," according to Steve Case.

Think this seems like the most obvious trait when comparing comeback cities to current startup hubs? You're right. Whether you're investing, trying to start a business, or just

---

54 Hensel, Anna. 2017. "Jeff Bezos, Eric Schmidt, and Others Give $150 Million to Steve Case's Middle America Startup Fund". *Venturebeat*. https://venturebeat.com/2017/12/04/jeff-bezos-eric-schmidt-and-others-give-150-million-to-steve-cases-middle-america-startup-fund/.

trying to live, comeback cities represent a financial opportunity not attainable in many other places.

CHAPTER 9

INDUSTRY INTEGRATION

According to Chris Olsen, "Value will come from marrying industry knowledge with technology[.] There's an arrogance in Silicon Valley that we don't need industry expertise. That's going to be less and less true in the future."[55]

I know this perspective. I lived it. Having spent years working in management consulting and having to explain that to family and friends who are engineers, electricians, medical professionals, and factory employees, the question I most frequently got was, "Why can't your clients just do it themselves? Don't they know their business better than you?"

The value of consulting as an industry is a conversation for a whole other book. This line of questioning from people

---

55   Lohr, Steve. "Midwest Beckons Tech Investors". 2017. *New York Times*. https://www.nytimes.com/2017/11/19/technology/midwest-tech-startups.html.

who are subject matter experts in their field in the most traditional sense, though, is a similarly appropriate line of questioning to pose to tech companies and software start-ups trying to solve highly specified industry problems from afar. This marriage of industry knowledge and technology is increasingly important, and it is driving innovation inland from the coasts.

Like a growing number of coastal venture capitalists leaving the coasts, former Sequoia Capital venture capitalist, Olsen, who co-founded Columbus-based Drive Capital in 2013, believes subject matter expertise in geographies that represent industrial giants of the past will be key moving forward. Former Silicon Valley venture capitalist, J.D. Vance, gained considerable attention when his homage to his roots, *Hillbilly Elegy: A Memoir of a Family and Culture in Crisis*, shot to the top of best seller lists in 2016. Since then, he has taken a similar path to Olsen, as a Managing Partner of Revolution's Rise of the Rest Seed Fund, and moved back to his home state of Ohio to start a nonprofit called Our Ohio Renewal. Some of the biggest names in venture capital from the west coast aren't moving to the Heartland for nothing.

They have seen that past industry is of the appeal of the entrepreneurial collaboration that is possible in comeback cities. Steve Case's book *The Third Wave: An Entrepreneur's Vision of the Future,* presents the idea that our society is entering phase three of the internet.

The first phase was its inception and adoption.

The second phase involved software and applications which were built on top of the internet.

The third phase we are entering will involve the total integration of connected internet into everything we do. He points specifically to industries such as health care, education, and agriculture as domains that will see the most consequential integration, industries that have dictated much of the transition period for comeback cities since major industries of the past disappeared.[56]

* * *

Like Boston has done, Baltimore has the opportunity to lead the way in healthcare innovation. Not only is it a wealth of talent and research due to educational and healthcare institutions such as Johns Hopkins University, University of Maryland, and University of Baltimore, but it is nearby the Washington-based research and regulatory agencies (Food and Drug Administration, National Institutes of Health,

---

56 Case, Steve. 2016. *The Third Wave: An Entrepreneur's Vision of the Future.* New York, NY: Simon and Schuster.

Centers for Medicare and Medicaid Services) that govern the highly regulated healthcare industry. Having this industrial knowledge base and proximity to regulators makes it the perfect place to marry the technology and acumen needed to navigate the medical field through the third wave.

Another comeback city that is poised to position itself at the center of innovation around one of the domains that will see considerable growth in technological integration is St. Louis. The region has an infrastructural lead in agricultural technology (agtech) because of the historic presence of Monsanto (company controversies around government lobbying and chemical product safety not withstanding). The talent generated from the University of Missouri and Washington University (St. Louis has more than 1,000 plant science PhD's—the highest concentration in the world), along with St. Louis's natural positioning around Missouri's abundance of fertile and developed farmland are also factors placing St. Louis at the center of agtech's future.

Advancements like the creation of 39 North, the state's first agtech innovation district, show that residents and entrepreneurs are not resting on the laurels of their city's past; instead, they are looking forward. 39 North is a roughly 600-acre district made up of many of the region's top agtech companies, disruptive startups in various stages of development, and the Helix Center Biotech Incubator for bioscience, agtech, and plant-science startups.[57] Couple the components of the growing startup ecosystem with the existing infrastructure, talent, and big corporations, and St. Louis has every chance to lead the way for agtech nationally.

Finally, Pittsburgh may be the most industry-agnostic city when it comes to key industry integration because of its recent positioning as a robotics hub. A collection of old warehouses and factories along the Allegheny River in the city's Strip District neighborhood make up what is known as Robotics Row. This tech corridor is host to a growing number of startup occupants fueled by the talent hotbed that Carnegie Mellon University's renowned engineering and computer science programs provide. The growing robotics ecosystem has formed a symbiotic relationship with some of the country's tech giants (Google, Uber, Facebook), attracting them to the Steel City because of its talent, infrastructure, and promise, while using their presence to draw national relevance to homegrown success stories.

Pittsburgh's manufacturing past and tech-heavy future make it the perfect place to form the intersection of robotics and key industries. Extensive research and development around

---

57   "39 North- St. Louis' New Agtech and Plant Science Innovation District". *St. Louis Economic Development Partnership.* 2019. https://stlpartnership.com/who-we-are/our-teams/39-north-agtech-district/.

robotics and automation has primed Pittsburgh to be the front-runner in bringing these technologies to local industries including agriculture, defense, health care, manufacturing, mining, transportation, and warehousing...precisely the industries that will be at the core of the internet's third wave.[58]

* * *

The related point to the third wave beyond industry integration is that partnerships will become even more important. As the internet and our connectedness to the technology around us continues to advance, citizens, companies, and institutions will increasingly need to collaborate to solve the world's most pressing challenges. Many of the largest companies in the previously mentioned key sectors are in these comeback cities. In Steve Case's mind, it's not just an opportunity, but it has become a necessity for the U.S. to maintain any competitive advantage that it has not already lost to other global power players.

"If you're not backing more of the entrepreneurs building companies in these places, there's a real risk that you miss out on what could be core differentiating capabilities in the third

---

58 Bitar, Eric. "Why Pittsburgh is Ideal for Robotics Businesses". 2017. *Robotics Business Review.* https://www.roboticsbusinessreview.com/manufacturing/pittsburgh-ideal-robotics-businesses/.

wave and it's likelier that those sectors will get disrupted by other countries."

Failing to lean on these resource-abundant cities and regions for the future that we anticipate would leave us unprepared to prosper from the technological innovations to come.

CHAPTER 10

ABUNDANCE OF BRAINS

"We used to export manufactured goods, but now unfortunately we export talented individuals."

Brain drain is a familiar concept to many. It involves the movement of highly educated or highly trained individuals from their place of origin to another. It has been a symptom of economic decline in comeback cities. For those who left and those who did not, it also creates psychological complications around feelings of "too good for home" for the former and feelings of "left behind" for the latter.

Home to two of our seven comeback cities, Ohio was hit particularly hard by the flight of talented young individuals seeking opportunities elsewhere. As of 2010, Ohio produced more bachelor's degrees per capita than the national average, but was a mere thirty-fifth in proportion of adults with a college degree, showing the stark difference in those who stay in Ohio or move to Ohio after their undergraduate education.[59]

On a positive note, the worst days of brain drain are behind us. A 2019 New York Times article by *Heartland* author Sarah Smarsh notes: "there is a brain gain afoot that suggests a national homecoming to less bustling places." She discusses the trend that the nation's most populous cities, New York City and Los Angeles, are losing population due to unaffordability, and people are making their way home—or to places like home that are more livable. She claims that in the past, "according to the American story, those who thrived in urban centers 'made it'—a capitalist triumph for the individual, a damaging loss for the place he left. We often refer to this as 'brain drain' from the hinterlands, implying that those who stay lack the merit or ability to 'get out.' " But this notion is getting dusty with each passing year.[60]

Although the worst days of brain drain may be in the past and, like the term Rust Belt itself, many find it overused, there are still hurdles to overcome to continue the trend

---

59 Marcus, Jon. 2010. *Times Higher Education.* http://www.highereducation.org/crosstalk/ctbook/pdfbook/OhioBrainDrainBookLayout.pdf

60 Smarsh, Sarah. "Something Special is Happening in Rural America". 2019. *New York Times.* https://www.nytimes.com/2019/09/17/opinion/rural-america.html?smid=nytcore-ios-share.

Smarsh wrote about. One of these is outlined in Andrew Yang's *Smart People Should Build Things*. In it, he talks about the path of those who have left their hometowns for prestigious universities across the country to eventually be caught up in the corporate recruiting complex, drawn by the allure of salary and prestige, the expectation of traditional success, and the skill set that encourages a continued traditional path. In 2007, forty-seven percent of all Harvard graduates went into either the consulting or finance industries. Even after a decline in this number resulting from the financial crisis, it was as high as thirty-six percent in 2017.[61] Seeing as the hubs for these industries are New York City, San Francisco, Boston, Chicago, Los Angeles, and Washington, the likelihood of those leaving comeback cities to pursue higher education only to come home and apply their skills is continually diminished.[62]

It doesn't have to be this way.

One of the biggest positives for comeback cities is the wealth of talent and resources available at universities, hospitals, and research institutions nearby upon which to build their futures. A 2016 book by investor Antoine van Agtmael and

61 Hopson, Chris. 2018. "The Draw of Consulting and Finance". *Harvard Political Review.* http://harvardpolitics.com/harvard/the-draw-of-consulting-and-finance/.

62 Yang, Andrew. 2014. *Smart People Should Build Things*. New York, NY: HarperBusiness.

journalist Fred Bakker called *The Smartest Places on Earth: Why Rustbelts Are the Emerging Hotspots of Global Innovation* describes the phenomenon of innovation-driven renewal in atypical regions for this kind of development.

Many of these growing hubs in the U.S. and Europe—dubbed Brainbelts—are in Rust Belt-like regions that have primary drivers, including universities and industry expertise. Bakker and van Agtmael toured many Brainbelt regions, focusing on:

- Raleigh-Durham-Chapel Hill (NC)
- Albany (NY), Akron (OH)
- Minneapolis-St. Paul (MN)
- Portland (OR)
- Eindhoven (Netherlands)
- Lundo-Malmö (Sweden)
- Oulu (Finland)
- Dresden (Germany)
- Zurich (Switzerland)

Each of these regions has its own growing area of expertise and at least one major research institution. Albany, for instance, is a hub for semiconductors and is home to Rensselaer Polytechnic Institute and SUNY Albany. The sharing of this brainpower across universities, researchers, entrepreneurs, and manufacturers in these belts is propelling these locations to a promising future.

> *With this new approach to creating smart products, then, Europe need not end up as a museum, the United States will not be pushed to the margin of the world map, and the creation of innovative twenty-first-century products need not be a zero-sum game [...] the list of the smartest places on earth will look very different in the years to come.*

Four of the comeback cities are considered to be Brainbelts. Pittsburgh's focus has been robotics and IT, supported by the science and engineering research and talent from Carnegie Mellon University. Buffalo has begun to develop as a hub for battery technology and clean energy, thanks in part to SUNY Buffalo. Detroit's Wayne State University has contributed to its development as a mobility and automation hub. St. Louis has been able to focus its innovation in bioscience and agtech with the brainpower supplied by Washington University and the University of Missouri, along with industry expertise from past companies and operations.[63] Cincinnati, Cleveland, and Baltimore each also have their own developing niches

---

63   Agtmael, Antoine van, and Fred Bakker. 2018. *The Smartest Places on Earth: Why Rustbelts are the Emerging Hotspots of Global Innovation.* New York, NY: PublicAffairs.

and considerable resources in the form of major universities, research institutions, and hospitals.

As described in the prior chapter on industry integration, the third wave of innovation that is upon us will involve full integration of connected technologies with our everyday lives. Part of the challenge of reaching the potential of this wave is the complexity of partnerships that will be needed across industries, political aisles, and geographic boundaries among other divides. Places like comeback cities and Brainbelts which will have been built upon the integration and collaboration between complex industries such as agriculture, health care, and energy will be paramount to the United States maintaining and furthering its position as a leader in global innovation.

* * *

The wealth of educational institutions in existence across comeback cities will be vital to the continued brain gain that is beginning to be seen. Talented young minds who grow up with a pride and sense of duty for their hometown must be cultivated by these educational institutions for them to recognize the value in entrepreneurial and community-focused endeavors instead of the corporate and traditionally safer versions of "successful" careers.

When visiting this topic of brain drain, brain gain, and the role of universities in growing a startup ecosystem within these cities, co-founder of Buffalo's first potential unicorn ACV Auctions, Jack Greco, found himself with a classic case of bird brain. Or, bird *on the brain,* to be precise:

Birds go out and by some black magic become pregnant. I say this because all the chatter on birds is around their mating dances and their nests of eggs and nothing on what happens in-between, so let's assume there is a wide spectrum of happenstance and circumstances that can lead to their pregnancy. A bird knows the maximum number of chicks she could have, just as our universities and research companies can count the number of viable students or team members that are present. However, she doesn't know 1) how well they are developing (just as we do not have clear markets to know how our students and working professionals are maturing as entrepreneurs) and 2) which and how many will hang around after they hatch.

Considerable care is given to the eggs until one day they hatch. At this point, they go from being fixed to a specific spot because of lack of ability (eggs cannot walk or fly or roll on their own volition like tumbleweeds) to unlimited ability. They have the power of flight, for goodness sake. As talent matures, it begins to have the ability to fly wherever it likes as well. Talent also does not keep local sentiment, as our institutions and schools in many cases do encapsulate people within their walls, embargoing exposure to anything but the inside of its institutional eggshell walls.

Thus all that a newborn bird and a developing student know is what the inside of that egg looks like. Had the bird's eggshell been fashioned with a small observation window to see what was happening in the world around as it was busy sprouting its first few feathers, it would have gained awareness to what may come next when the time comes to leave the nest. It would benefit from watching its mother forage for food, rebuild the nest, and interact with other birds. At the same time, it would also hold a deep appreciation for the very spot it was maturing and understanding of the local landscape, a familiarity that breeds connection. Now when our dear baby bird hatched, it would not only have a visual understanding to match up with its instinctual movements, but would have grown an attachment to the local area and saw the feasibility to remaining local.

We all were birds and where we lived was viable for those that raised us. Because of a lack of interaction with the world we would enter as talented and trained adult professionals, though, some did not view it as viable.

We lacked the native awareness that could have been instilled in parallel to our educational maturation a regional knowledge and platform for experimentation while we were still tied to the nest. This nest—a home or university setting—could have allowed us to connect with the entrepreneurial community, gain appreciation and link to resources, mentors, and kindred spirits. In turn, we could begin to dream and build and get comfortable with the idea that this is as good a place as any to take employment, settle a family, and start a new opportunity.

For something to drain, it needed to exist in the first place, so the name of the game is retention, but more specifically, retention with a purpose, an intelligent plan, that reciprocates by adding to a verdant ecosystem that now boasts another creature to interact, attract and collide with those still developing.

The integration of the gold mine that universities represent in comeback cities into the startup ecosystem will be essential in tapping into the asset that these educational institutions represent. In doing so, the fledgling birds being incubated by universities will have a chance to peer outside of their eggshell and be equipped to fly to impressive heights around their nest.

No more bird analogies, I promise.

CHAPTER 11

BIG COMPANIES = BIG HELP

———

Self-preservation is a prevailing force of human nature; not only a will to survive, but to protect one's position and power. This self-preservation is an inclination that seems in direct opposition to another overwhelming force that tends to grow as individuals progress in their personal and professional life: to provide mentorship and guidance to up-and-comers with little expectation of benefit.

For the betterment of society, I am happy to see that the latter force tends to win out as often as it does, particularly in thriving startup communities. This desire to pass on experience and wisdom is especially important when talking about building entrepreneurship capabilities in a city. When looking at comeback cities, a commonality that comes from their shared success during a period when many of today's Fortune 500 companies were getting off the ground is the continued presence of these big companies.

Despite self-preservation and defending the bottom line being even more evident when talking about an existing large company, the importance of their mentorship to new companies is one of the most crucial cogs in an entrepreneurial ecosystem. Brad Feld's *Startup Communities* identifies the most powerful things large companies can do for startups as "[providing] a convening space and resources for local startups, [and creating] programs to encourage startups to build companies that enhance the large company's ecosystem."[64]

While these are powerful actions large companies can take, there are other helping hands that they can lend which will not only bolster startup activity, but also benefit them as the greater economy, talent pool, and area recognition increase from collective success. This requires a big picture perspective that is not always easy for corporations to see. At the surface, big companies see competition. But thinking about their existence in the local and regional ecosystem, contributing to the growth of startups is a net positive for them in terms of talent, partnerships, investment, and interest.

* * *

64 Feld, Brad, and David Kaplan. 2012. *Startup Communities: Building an Entrepreneurial Ecosystem in Your City.* Hoboken, NJ: John Wiley and Sons, Inc.

The city of Cincinnati is a prime example of the benefits that can occur when this perspective is adopted by existing companies. In late 2011, it was announced that global foods producer and former Fortune 500 company, Chiquita Brands International, was accepting a $22 million offer to move its headquarters from Cincinnati to Charlotte, NC, after the state of Ohio was unable to make a matching incentive offer. For Cincinnati, the move meant not only 300 well-paying jobs leaving the area, but another dent in its national and global relevance as it continues to fight its way out of the economic decline it had faced for decades.[65]

This move was enormous for the Cincinnati business community, and warranted an equally massive effort to counteract its effects. The Cincinnati Business Committee, a board of executives from regional Fortune 500 companies, took it upon themselves to think big and view the region's economy as a collective challenge to solve with a long-term plan. One of the major outcomes of this collective effort was the creation of Cintrifuse, "a public-private partnership established by the big companies themselves to foster the next phase of

---

65 Levingston, Chelsey. "Chiquita Gets $22 Million To Move Headquarters to Charlotte ". 2011. *Dayton Daily News*. https://www.daytondailynews.com/news/local/chiquita-gets-million-move-headquarters-charlotte/S7ayK3KcL8pSihJm573j3H/.

economic growth for Cincinnati: technology and innovation delivered by startups."[66]

Created in a partnership with the City of Cincinnati and EY, Cintrifuse has multiple components to feed the regional entrepreneurial ecosystem. One of which is the Cintrifuse Syndicate Fund which invests in venture capital firms outside of the region with no requirement that they invest in Cincinnati startups, but an understanding that they create a regional engagement plan to ensure their involvement in the regional ecosystem.

Former Cintrifuse CEO, Wendy Lea, was recruited to help Cincinnati's startup ecosystem grow. Having no substantial ties to the area, she was understandably hesitant. Talk to her now, though, and it is clearly a city she feels a strong connection to. The work they accomplished is one of her proudest achievements. She'll be the first to admit that much of the city's success came from involving big companies in the area as mentors and supporters to local startups.

Lea described the magnitude of this step, "Cincinnati has more Fortune 500 companies than anywhere else outside of

---

66 Weissmann, Eric. "Creating an Ecosystem: Who Benefits When Big Companies Work with Startups?". 2018. *Forbes*. https://www. forbes.com/sites/forbescommunicationscouncil/2018/08/14/ creating-an-ecosystem-who-benefits-when-big-companies-work-with-startups/#6c46cd12539f.

San Francisco Bay area, so we created a Customer Connections program to share information between large companies and small companies."[67]

Sharing connections with big companies allows for startups to take advantage of experienced leader mentorship, stay abreast of the broader pressing business problems and solutions, and work collaboratively to attract the best talent to the region. However, it wasn't as simple as making a phone call to 1-800-BIG-COMP and asking for help.

Cincinnati was able to make these connections happen thanks to a couple of key steps taken by Lea and her team. First, branding efforts alongside StartupCincy as the Greater Cincinnati Startup Community, instead of focusing on the name Cintrifuse, made a difference in getting many important players involved. When it felt less like a competition and more like a collaboration to move forward together, eyes seemed to open up to the idea.

Second, Lea took the approximately 140 "BigCos" or existing sizable companies and reached out to find out who each company's visionary was. It wasn't about getting every Chief

---

67 Nash-Hoff, Michele. 2016. "Cincinnati's Cintrifuse Connects Entrepreneurs, Big Companies and Tech Funds". *Industry Week*. https://www.industryweek.com/innovation/cincinnatis-cintrifuse-connects-entrepreneurs-big-companies-and-tech-funds.

Technology Officer or Chief Innovation Officer involved. Instead, it was about finding the *right* person to get involved. Oftentimes, it was someone more junior than you may anticipate, but it was someone the CEO relied upon when thinking about the company's future. Taking these steps of finding the right champions within big companies and making everyone feel like they are in this effort together are key for any city's collective endeavor.

Comeback cities have an inherent advantage over entrepreneurial communities starting from scratch in that department. Many of these cities have multiple Fortune 500 companies to engage in the building process. The size and collective spirit of each comeback city's region allows them to engage at a more comprehensive level than startups in much larger cities, and should be taken advantage of as part of overall regional development. To waste the opportunity of finding mentorship in existing firms is detrimental to the startup because of the knowledge, experience, and resources available to them. At the same time, the larger company is missing out on the new and innovative ideas that startups are constantly churning out, many of which can also come to impact their existing business in positive ways.

PART 3

CULTURAL TRAITS: LOVE, CONNECTION, AND REALISM

"It's a twisted love that runs the gamut of emotions: Joy, disappointment, hurt, anger, fear, elation, delight, apprehension, courage, resentment, cynicism, stubbornness, optimism and confusion...But when it's love, you know it's real."

—*AARON FOLEY*

* * *

Remember before when I brought up the concept of goodwill in accounting? When an acquiring company purchases another company and pays more than the book value of that company, the difference is accounted for as the amount of goodwill. Goodwill, in and of itself, is an intangible asset, but to think about it conceptually, it represents the sum of any number of other intangible assets that a company might pay more or less than book value based upon. For instance, if there is a strong market at the time of acquisition, or there is a strong brand name, this could be captured in the amount of goodwill paid.

What am I getting at here? The cultural traits that continually come up among comeback cities can be thought of like goodwill. You may not be able to touch the productivity of a company's employees like you would a piece of its machinery, but that productivity certainly has value. Similarly, there are certain cultural traits engrained in each of the comeback cities that—whether I can see them or not—would lead me to bet high on makers and builders that come from these places.

Cultural traits identified as common traits across comeback cities include:

1. Love of place—the pride and connection comeback city residents feel for their city is a special motivator for entrepreneurial success.
2. Collegiality and connection—the personal and familial connections between people in comeback cities provides

a level of focus on community prosperity unparalleled in other places.

3. Fatalism, realism, and optimism—with the difficulties of decades past, people in these cities are realists and pragmatists, but more importantly they are eternally optimistic even in the face of economic depression.

4. No fake it 'til you make it—comeback city residents value things that are tangible, making it a place that has the potential to spur real, revenue-generating companies for investors.

5. Eager for a winning culture—having been starved of any regular success stories in the recent past, comeback cities are hungry to back and support any wins in the community.

6. Limited options then, unlimited potential now—these places were marked by only a few manufacturing employers in the past, so to unlock a whole new menu of options for employment would unleash unlimited potential.

CHAPTER 12

LOVE OF PLACE

―――

Topophilia—from the Greek *topos* "place" and *-philia,* "love of"—is just that. It is love of place, or place attachment, in which an individual's identity and culture are irrevocably linked. Geographer Yi-Fu Tuan defines it as the "emotional connections between physical environment and human beings."[68] I knew people in comeback cities would be familiar with this feeling, this intense love of place, because virtually everyone I've met from these places exudes it whether they mean to or not.

By no means do I mean to diminish the pride and love that people have for cities outside the seven we are looking at, but there is something fervent about the way a Pittsburgher or a Clevelander talks about their city. Heaven forbid a couple of expat Clevelanders cross paths in another city. That would

―――

68   "Topophilia". 2019. *Stamps School of Art and Design.* https://stamps.umich.edu/exhibitions/detail/topophilia.

be a lovefest for the ages. Why this is the case is not totally clear. I would be willing to bet that part of this love of place is a bit of a defense mechanism. From personal experience, people from comeback cities spend more time defending their city to others who just don't seem to understand than those from other places.

The City of Detroit's chief storyteller Aaron Foley, appointed by Mayor Mike Duggan, penned an essay that illustrates much of what comeback city residents feel about their home titled "We Love Detroit, Even if You Don't". A couple excerpts capture topophilia to a "T":

> Detroit is a lot of things. It is not the small town you grew up in, where you went to a crappy high school in the country and dreamed daily of flying the coop to New York City or Hollywood. It is, by and large, still a city where people migrate, or maintain [...]

> Detroit didn't need a bankruptcy filing to tell us we were broke because we already knew. It's an enigmatic tangled web in the darkest abyss that takes more than a Slate piece here or a CNN panel there to explain. Still, I'll attempt a TL;DR [Too Long; Didn't Read]: A crowded city full of a rising middle class that reached its peak when freeways provided access to spacious land beyond city limits. A crowded city that also faced rising tensions

between black residents and white residents. Redlining. Access. Police brutality. Draining economic resources. Unequal pay. Riots. Rising costs. Dwindling tax base. Legacy costs incurred by pensions, unions, city services. Inflation. Industry collapse. Taxes. Corruption. Crime. Schools. Jobs, and the lack of them. All against the backdrop of a shitty American economy in general.

I live in Detroit. It's hot as hell right now and we're having biblical rainstorms. Grass is growing like crazy. But you know, I see people cutting the grass on lots that aren't theirs. Every day when I pass through my neighborhood on my way to work.

I see little old ladies tending to their annuals, kids — black and white — playing football in the street (even though they can be annoying because they block the street sometimes). I see a bunch of regular-ass people doing regular-ass shit because Detroit is a regular-ass city with regular-ass problems just like everyone else.

Which is why I wholeheartedly believe that Detroit will be just fine.

[...] I love Detroit, I know a ton of people who love Detroit. It's a twisted love that runs the gamut of emotions: joy, disappointment, hurt, anger, fear, elation, delight,

apprehension, courage, resentment, cynicism, stubborn-
ness, optimism and confusion. Then again, maybe that's
something we all have in common. Have you ever loved?
You mean to tell me that everything you've loved was just
cut and clear? There was never any condition or obstacle?

But when it's love, you know it's real. And love conquers
all, even the stigma of Chapter 9 bankruptcy and the
national head-shaking that's coming with it. So yeah,
Detroit will be just fine. Even if you don't think so.[69]

Foley's words *speak to me*. People ask me about Buffalo
often. To my friends from places all over the country, I am
their only Buffalo connection. They know I have what they
consider to be a weird obsession. They are good friends and
try to take an interest by asking about the Bills, forwarding
any news story that mentions the city, and giving me credit
whenever I forget to wear a warm jacket because I'm used
to those Buffalo winters. They are great friends, but I know
they think it's weird.

The few times that they've really wanted to dive into why
I care so much about Buffalo, even without any near-term
plans to live there again, I've gone off. "The people are one
of a kind," I'll start.

---

69 Foley, Aaron. "We Love Detroit, Even If You Don't". 2013. *Jalopnik*.
    https://jalopnik.com/we-love-detroit-even-if-you-dont-832204589.

I am slamming my fingertips extra hard as I type each letter because I can't convey it any better than that and it's frustrating. Sure, everything you hear about the winters are true, but we are ravenous hometown supporters *despite* that. That should tell you something. I'll go on and on about history, sports, architecture, food, music, and a million other reasons why Buffalo is great. Typically, there isn't much back and forth because whoever I'm speaking to doesn't have the Buffalo knowledge or interest to go much further.

"That's so awesome that you love where you're from so much."

That's usually how it ends.

"Yeah, man."

I turn away and move on with my day, smiling, because I know they'll never understand. And, frankly, I don't care. I hear you, Aaron.

＊ ＊ ＊

Mary Grove, a partner with Revolution's Rise of the Rest Seed Fund, noticed this same feeling in many of the cities traveled to on their bus tour to award seed money to promising startups throughout the "rest" of America outside of Boston, New York City, and San Francisco. She described it as a feeling of hunger and fierce loyalty, echoing many of the sentiments above. This loyalty is not just to their own family and friends, but to their city which they have been left to defend from outsiders and naysayers.

From an entrepreneurial perspective, this unparalleled topophilia that exists in comeback cities is one of its best and most encouraging traits. It is the primary reason that I, having felt it my whole life, am rock-solid, don't-bother-arguing, certain-as-can-be that these cities have a bright future waiting to be seen.

Talking to venture capitalists in these cities, one of the most common answers I received to the question of what characteristics do you look for in a founder, was that they need to have the desire to truly *own* the problem that their idea or company sets out to solve. This sense of ownership would be the clearest sign that this individual would do everything within their power to succeed. Oftentimes, the problem a founder is trying to solve has surfaced because they've faced it in their own life or seen it in their own community. As such, there is a level of responsibility that the founder feels not just to themselves, but to their community and to their *place* to solve the problem. Feeling accountable and feeling like you are always a representative of your entire city is surely a healthy dose of motivation for any entrepreneur.

This isn't the first instance of community pride and accountability being a catalyst for entrepreneurialism. When researching why Silicon Valley outperformed Route 128 in Massachusetts, UC Berkeley professor, Anno Saxenian, found that many of the engineers in the early decades (1970s and 1980s) said that they felt like they "worked for Silicon Valley" rather than for any single company. This strong regional identification was an important part of the early culture that supported the Valley's success. I believe it can serve a similar purpose for comeback cities.

* * *

Love of place is all well and good, but not pragmatically valuable if the brain drain of these comeback cities continues. On a positive note, this trend seems to have reversed as many who left for work and education are returning home, or "boomeranging" as they see new hope in their native cities. Although specific return migration statistics are unavailable, Pittsburgh recently reversed the decades long trend of out-migration among eighteen- to twenty-four-year-olds and saw its first year of overall population growth in 2013 for the first time since its heyday. Other comeback cities such as Detroit, St. Louis, and Cleveland have also seen recent population growth, much of which stems from young people moving to, and in some cases returning to live in these cities.[70] Cities that draw this kind of devotion run much less risk of being a flash in the pan success, particularly when they are able to draw in talent that has left or—more optimistically—eventually prevent talented young people from leaving to begin with.

Along with boomerang talent, the pride and love that people have for their comeback city extends to those who have left, found financial success elsewhere and want to return their hard-earned money to their city. These represent the assets that have yet to be fully realized by comeback cities. In Detroit, majority owner of the Cleveland Cavaliers, Quicken Loans founder, and Rock Ventures founder, Dan Gilbert, not only moved Quicken Loans downtown in his hometown of Detroit, but he has committed to invest over one billion dollars in buildings around the city. He also founded Detroit Venture Partners to invest in local tech startups. This emotional attachment to these cities is a driving force for the development that has happened and that which is still to occur.[71]

---

70 Harrison, Jill. "Rust Belt Boomerang: The Pull of Place in Moving Back to a Legacy City". 2017. *City & Community*. https://www. researchgate.net/publication/319104431_Rust_Belt_Boomerang_ The_Pull_of_Place_in_Moving_Back_to_a_Legacy_City

71 Henderson, Tom. "Heavyweight Investors Join Dan Gilbert in New VC Fund in Detroit". 2016. *Crain's Detroit Business*. https:// www.crainsdetroit.com/article/20160111/NEWS/160119974/ heavyweight-investors-join-dan-gilbert-in-new-vc-fund-in-detroit.

A method for making the most of these expats love of place is what *Startup Community Way* co-author Ian Hathaway refers to as building a diaspora:

> *People leave these places for any number of reasons—self-discovery, employment opportunities, following or finding a partner, and so on—but choose to remain connected, in some way, to their roots. Perhaps they even maintain the hope of returning one day when the time is right. What is overlooked among these short-term "losses," is the potential for what is learned "out there" to have significant value for the community back home, if properly cultivated.*

> *In the context of building startup ecosystems, this is doubly true, where the process of starting and scaling high-growth businesses is niche, and best learned at an arm's length (learning by doing/seeing). This is why places like Silicon Valley continue to attract talent, even as the practicalities of living there seem to be untenable—the resources, the culture, the tacit knowledge, all make the congestion and exorbitant cost of living worth it.*

> *And yet, with the right mindset, what's learned there can be transferred elsewhere.*[72]

---

72 Hathaway, Ian. 2017. "Feeling Isolated? Build a Diaspora". *Ian Hathaway*. http://www.ianhathaway.org/blog/2017/6/6/

In her 2006 book, *The New Argonauts: Regional Advantage in a Global Economy*, Anno Saxenian of UC Berkeley chronicles how foreign-born engineers and managers working in Silicon Valley were able to transfer localized knowledge—on how to build and invest in scalable technology ventures—back to their home countries. She specifically points to a critical mass of motivated Taiwanese and Israelis in the 1980s, and Chinese and Indians in the 1990s, as essential to the burgeoning innovation ecosystems we see in those places today:[73]

Some of these migrants stayed as expats, others returned home, while others still migrated to California to replace those leaving. What was common among them was their connection to home and a desire to bring what was learned abroad back there. Instead of Silicon Valley as a central source of "brain drain," a group of motivated, patriotic, opportunistic individuals became a pipeline of "brain circulation"—where invaluable knowledge obtained at the frontier of technology and entrepreneurship was transferred back home, planting the seeds of the next generation of booming global innovation that followed [...] don't ignore those who have left, or resort to a sense of frustration at the inability to "keep talent at home." Instead, view it as an opportunity. Build stronger ties with your diaspora, learn from them,

feeling-isolated-build-a-diaspora?rq=diaspora.

73 Saxenian, AnnaLee. 2007. *The New Argonauts: Regional Advantage in a Global Economy*. Harvard University Press.

engage with them, keep them emotionally tied to the region and interested in its success. Some may return to live there—be prepared for them. Others may choose not to return. But make sure they, too, have constructive ways of engaging with the startup community there—as mentors, investors, or advisors.[74]

Across many comeback cities, efforts to do exactly this are underway. Events often called some variation of "Homecoming" are being hosted more frequently. At the time of this book's publishing, Detroit has hosted five annual homecoming events, Baltimore has hosted two, and Buffalo has hosted one. Detroit's annual homecoming events alone have directly yielded over $400 million in investments and commitments for Detroit.[75]

In these cities, groups are actively working to understand and engage these expats to determine what their current and desired relationship with their hometown is. Whether that relationship ends up being a direct investment into new companies back home, or simply a form of ongoing mentorship from those who have been successful entrepreneurs

74 Hathaway, Ian. 2017. "Feeling Isolated? Build a Diaspora". *Ian Hathaway*. http://www.ianhathaway.org/blog/2017/6/6/ feeling-isolated-build-a-diaspora?rq=diaspora.

75 "Detroit Homecoming Expats Invest in Their Hometown". 2019. *Crain's Detroit Business*. https:// www.crainsdetroit.com/detroit-homecoming/ detroit-homecoming-expats-invest-their-hometown.

elsewhere, their involvement is a crucial way to tap into the unique tool of topophilia. There will be no magic bullet, no Facebook group that will keep expats easily engaged; instead, success will come from a thousand nudges and touchpoints from those committed to building a self-sustaining startup community that can be a driver of economic development.

This concept is being put into practice for comeback cities by places like Buffalo, creating chapters of entrepreneurial expats in cities around the country to keep them plugged into their hometown. By mentoring, opening their network, connecting with other Buffalonians in their current cities, or even investing, these expats are reconnecting with their hometown despite not being able to return there for good.

What kinds of U.S. cities could really get away with cold-calling people and asking them to give their time to strangers back home?

Probably just these ones.

CHAPTER 13

COLLEGIALITY AND CONNECTION

———

One of Brad Feld's necessary attributes of leadership in a startup community is to play a non-zero-sum game. What this means is that there does not have to be winners and losers; there is enough growth and opportunity for everyone to win.

This mind-set is one that lends itself to the collegiality necessary to truly develop an ecosystem. A #givefirst mind-set, if you will. One of the cultural components of comeback cities that provides an inherent advantage is a built-in sense of collegiality, partially due to the nontransient nature of these cities and partially due to the shared struggle of economic downturn.

Living in Washington, DC for the past few years, there are few American cities that have more of a transient feel. To my friends who were born and raised in the DC area who are already starting to bristle, I know you're there and you're passionate about your hometown. I am, for the sake of comparing cities, generalizing.

But also, you can't compare to comeback cities. I'm kidding!

Maybe.

I've heard individuals—particularly those in their twenties and thirties—who have been in DC for only a handful of years begin to call themselves pseudo-natives because they have a longer-standing bond with the city compared with many other young people who are in and out within a few years. According to a 2015 study, Washington ranked fourth out of the fifty most populated cities in the country in the percentage of population that moved away in the past year at 7.7 percent.

On the opposite end of the spectrum was Buffalo in last place with just under 3.5 percent. Many of the other comeback cities have similarly low rates of people moving away, including Detroit at just 4.7 percent despite its overall steep population loss throughout the 1990s and early 2000s.[76] While the

---

76 "Popular Cities in America: Where People are Moving to Fastest ". 2016. *ABODO Apartments.* https://www.abodo.com/blog/so-long-to-the-city/.

initial impression may be that low migration rates in comeback cities are from positives economic variables such as an increased number of jobs available, there is also a historic nontransient nature within these cities to consider. Although the trend is less so than in past decades, someone is more likely to remain in their hometown comeback city for the entirety of their lives than in most other major metropolitan areas.

I don't mean to diminish any sense of pride or make a larger comparison between where I live now (Washington) and where I've lived in the past (Buffalo, Pittsburgh, Baltimore), but there is a marked difference in the immediate connection between someone who has Baltimore or Buffalo ties compared to the lack of enthusiasm shown if I meet someone with DC ties somewhere else around the country or around the world.

It happens multiple times per week for me. I'm in Washington or any other city and I see someone with a Buffalo-related shirt or hat on. I approach with an instinctual "Go Bills" which is quickly reciprocated before we dive into the "how many questions before we find a close, shared connection" game. Usually it starts with narrowing your hometown to the city of Buffalo, the Southtowns or Northtowns. From there, we each filter our mental rolodex and start naming schools, churches, and employers of our family and friends in that area.

If the other person is willing to play this game to completion, I think I am batting near .1000. And, perhaps a bit more oddly, I would put the batting average of how often this brief encounter with a stranger ends in a hug over .500 as well.

Coming from tight-knit communities leads to a sense of collegiality unrivaled by bigger or more transient cities. This collegiality draws from connections that transcend professional roles, many of which are familial or come from shared friends. Another important aspect of successful startup communities, per Feld, is the willingness to engage the entire entrepreneurial stack. Those that make up this entrepreneurial stack include first-time entrepreneurs, experienced entrepreneurs, aspiring entrepreneurs, investors, mentors, employees of startups, government, universities, service providers, and large existing companies.[77] With cooperation across these multifaceted organizations and individuals being a key component of city- or region-wide success, having a built-in culture of connection and collegiality immediately gives comeback cities a sturdy base upon which to build.

---

77 Feld, Brad, and David Kaplan. 2012. *Startup Communities: Building an Entrepreneurial Ecosystem In Your City*. Hoboken, NJ: John Wiley and Sons, Inc.

One caveat on the collegiality of comeback cities that cannot be overstated is the underlying racial and social divides raised in the prior chapter on broader issues. While this trait of comeback cities is advantageous, it does not transcend deeper divides which must continue to be addressed for this character trend to touch all pockets of these cities.

These comeback cities, like most others around the country, still maintain a certain level of "old boys club" that the startup community must seek to work with and work past if lasting changes are to be made.

* * *

A book called *Start-up Nation: The Story of Israel's Economic Miracle*, written by Dan Senor and Paul Singer, examines how the relatively tiny nation of Israel has become the world's per capita leader in innovation and entrepreneurialism. In 2008, Israel's 7.1 million people received close to $2 billion in venture capital, the same amount received by the 145 million people in Germany and France combined.[78]

The premise is that the two main factors in Israel's collective economic success are mandatory military service and immigration. The former drives innovation for a number of

78 Senor, Dan, and Saul Singer. 2011. *Start-Up Nation*. Toronto: McClelland & Stewart.

reasons, including the nonhierarchical environment of the Israeli Defense Forces and the wide variety of skills young Israelis are able to develop during their service. Immigration contributes to overall economic success because, Israel is inherently made up of immigrants and their descendants, resulting in a culture that embraces risk and entrepreneurship. Immigrants have historically started businesses at a far higher rate than nonimmigrants (in the U.S. in 2016 alone, immigrants were exactly twice as likely to start a business as a U.S.-born adult in any given month).[79]

It is, without a doubt, worth reading in its entirety, but the reason this book is relevant to our point around collegiality and connection in comeback cities is one that was not delved into deeply in *Start-up Nation*, but alluded to. In it, Senor and Singer interview Colonel John Lowry, a marine infantry officer who went on to get his MBA from Harvard Business School before climbing the corporate ranks at Harley Davidson. Lowry discusses his desire that the lessons he gained from his military experience were as common in the U.S. business world as they are in Israel's: "The military gets you at a young age and teaches you that when you are in charge of something, you are responsible for everything that

79 Kosten, Dan. "Immigrants as Economic Contributors: Immigrant Entrepreneurs". 2018. *National Immigration Forum.* https://immigrationforum.org/article/immigrants-as-economic-contributors-immigrant-entrepreneurs/.

happens...and everything that does not happen. The phrase 'It was not my fault' does not exist in the military culture."[80]

This quote got me thinking about the role of accountability in entrepreneurship. In a vacuum, entrepreneurs are working on their own for their company and their customers. When their environment dictates another level of accountability for, say, their entire community, the stakes have just gotten considerably higher.

The willingness and ease with which comeback city natives and enthusiasts find connections with one another lends itself not only to a shared motivation, but also a substantial level of accountability. As the cases of the cultures created in the U.S. Marine Corps and Israeli Defense Forces illustrate, shared feeling of responsibility for outcomes result in more dedicated, thoughtful, and strategic business leaders.

If comeback cities are able to tap into the accountability that comes with a feeling of connectedness to your community, they have the potential to see results like that of Israel's innovative culture.

80 Senor, Dan, and Saul Singer. 2011. *Start-Up Nation*. Toronto: McClelland & Stewart.

CHAPTER 14

FATALISM, REALISM, AND OPTIMISM

———

"Part of the personality of these cities is that the glass isn't just half empty, but someone *stole* the glass."

Chris Heivly used this to describe the "feel" in comeback cities when prompted to do so. At first glance, you might think this is harsh. Although he continued by saying that this feeling is not representative nor does it paint the whole picture of the fallout of a group of cities' complex histories, I would argue that there is definitely some validity.

I consider myself a staunch defender of all things delipidated cities. Acknowledging that the cities I love are not what you would call "classically handsome" is the first step to putting myself on equal footing with those I'm talking to. They know I'm not a delusional person, so they are more likely to actually hear what I have to say when I rattle off the quirks and intricacies that make me love the city I'm from and those with which I share a kinship more than they could possibly understand.

At the same time, the gallows humor that often serves as a defense mechanism can unknowingly yield a sense of fatalism that acts as a restrictor for any attempted comeback. Fatalism can destroy initiative. When a manufacturing mill that employs a sizeable portion of a city's population shuts down because of complex macroeconomic forces, it feels like your way of life is under attack, but there is no enemy to fight. You cannot grasp the problem when it looms larger than the individual, the company, the neighborhood, or even the players in city hall. When decline and stagnation have reigned for multiple decades and no one has been able to figure out the specific things that went wrong to right them, fatalism sets in.

I often wonder, though, if I'm doing a disservice by admitting defeat to some degree, and acknowledging the negative perception of these often forgotten places. But then I remember that nobody who loves these places would ever try to ignore the realities that make them special in so many ways. This realism, in a sense, is one of the cornerstones of each comeback city citizen's psyche. It gives way to the many traits that these same individuals take pride in: grit, humility, and resilience.

These are precisely the traits that give me hope for comeback cities. Sure, these cities have an outer crust of fatalism from their generation(s) of tough times, but give them a reason to believe and their optimism is unrelenting. I would argue that there are even more instances in which these cities exude unshaking optimism in the face of adversity than they do a sense of "somebody stole the glass."

* * *

A study in the Journal of Personality and Social Psychology does support this feeling that Heivly described, though. The study conducted collaboratively between psychologists, historians, and economic geographers, looked into whether there was a link between individual former industrial regions in the United Kingdom and the U.S. and increased markers of "psychological adversity" (e.g., higher neuroticism, lower conscientiousness, lower aspects of extraversion, lower life satisfaction, and lower life expectancy). The research shows that "a region's historical industries leave a lasting imprint on the local psychology, which remains even when those industries are no longer dominant or have almost completely disappeared."[81] This causal link is certainly negative at face value, but that is only a small part of these cities' personalities.

---

81 Obschonka, Martin. "Research: The Industrial Revolution Left Psychological Scars that Can Still be Seen Today". 2018. *Harvard Business Review.* https://hbr.org/2018/03/

Let's get to the positives of this psyche.

More importantly, these places have an underlying sense of belief, hope, and optimism that despite the woes of the past, things will turn out okay because the strength of the people and their love of place is powerful. This dichotomy of fatalism and practical idealism are well-represented in some of the most common nicknames for these comeback cities.

Cleveland has been called the "Mistake on the Lake" by outsiders, but natives would quickly correct you that you're talking about "Believeland." Buffalo is both the "City of No Illusions" while taking pride in being the "City of Good Neighbors." Baltimore's violence once earned it the reputation of "Bodymore, Murdaland," but the its optimism has led to the title of "America's Comeback City." No offense to the other comeback cities.

This psyche still has roots from generations of loss, but these communities are eager to latch onto and shout small victories from the top of their tallest building.

What comes to mind when I say the words "Kan Jam" to you? You might say to yourself, "What is this guy talking about? I thought jam was usually jarred, not canned." You

research-the-industrial-revolution-left-psychological-scars-that-can-still-be-seen-today.

might know the yard game I'm referring to and picture the black plastic cans and neon yellow frisbees. But if you're from Buffalo, you're probably going to get all riled up and make sure I know that this award winner for world's best backyard game (according to me) was invented in Buffalo.

How do I know that you would do this if you were from Buffalo? Because I do it. I'm that guy.

It is quite literally a converted trash can and a frisbee. You throw one at the other and try to hit it—a simple concept. That won't stop myself or any other Buffalonians from being proud of it. We don't need much, just give us a reason to sing the city's praises and you will not hear the end of it.

* * *

Beyond sports, cities like Baltimore are proud of new development projects and see influential individuals and public masses rally around them with remarkable enthusiasm. Port Covington in South Baltimore is developing what will be dubbed Cyber Town, USA. This development project aims to stake Baltimore as a hub for creation and entrepreneurship in cybersecurity. The effort has gained considerable momentum locally, and has been widely lauded by politicians at the local, state, and federal level.

According to Congressman Dutch Ruppersberger, "The expansion and relocation of these firms to Port Covington only helps solidify Baltimore and Maryland's reputation as the cybersecurity capital of the world. I am thankful for this investment and excited to see the talent and economic domino-effect this could bring to the entire region."[82]

The Cyber Town effort has also been supported by investors around the region and Baltimore behemoth Under Armour. The unique aspect of cities like Baltimore is that the enthusiasm felt by those within the startup and cybersecurity community for a project like this is matched by the broader public—not because they are particularly involved in this world, but because they represent Baltimore and Baltimore represents them, so any advancement is felt at the individual level.

This expectation of failure that has permeated comeback city communities for so long is a negative that not only can be offset, but can be outweighed by the countering optimism, enthusiasm, and communal support from these cities when they do have something to celebrate.

Just give them a reason and you'll see.

---

82 West, Rebecca & Gast, Jenn. "Port Covington Set to Become a Global Cybersecurity Hub". 2019. *PRWEB*. https://www.prweb.com/releases/port_covington_set_to_become_a_global_cybersecurity_hub/prweb15845771.htm.

CHAPTER 15

NO FAKE IT 'TIL YOU MAKE IT

———

A recent Planet Money podcast caught my ear. Granted, most of them do, but this one in particular did because it spoke of what I deem to be a groundbreaking take on a massive societal problem. The episode discussed student loan debt— one of the biggest problems facing young (and a growing population of old) people today.

Purdue University has created an alternative to scholarships and traditional private or federal student loans: Income Share Agreements. The basic premise is that students will agree to give a certain percentage of their future earnings for a fixed number of years, rather than pay a set dollar amount. The more successful they are, the more successful the investing fund is. If they struggle to find promising employment, they won't be crippled.[83]

---

83 "903: A New Way to Pay for College". 2019. Podcast. *Planet Money.*

Despite this concept being fascinating for its own merits as a response to the student loan crisis, I couldn't help but think of comeback cities. Let me take it back a step and explain.

"Fake it 'til you make it doesn't really play here."

When prompted to describe the types of entrepreneurs and companies they look for in their particular city, comeback city investors described experience, determination, and a prove-it mentality. Many local angel investors have helped to set this tone, as privately wealthy individuals in these cities, when compared to many other cities around the country, have traditionally made their fortune based on the success and profits of manufacturing companies.

Their money is hard-earned and they are hard-pressed to give it to just anybody.

Many of comeback cities' affluent individuals have been less knowledgeable about the technologies being developed elsewhere, and thus, have been less inclined to become angel investors in these types of startups. Angel investor risk can be offset when groups of angel investors create a syndicate or angel group and invest together, but unlike the naturally occurring entrepreneurial ecosystems in places like Silicon Valley, angel groups in comeback cities likely need to be organized by a third party to really take shape.

For this reason, you will not see many individual investors willing to bet on an idea or a concept.[84] While this can be a limiting factor from an individual perspective, if you look at it from an entrepreneurial ecosystem perspective, there are benefits to developing a community of founders who approach their company with an "I need to really prove that this thing works" mind-set.

* * *

Back to our Purdue University Income Share Agreement discussion. If I was contributing to the fund investing in Purdue University students, what are the kinds of things I would look for? Test scores, leadership, and extracurricular experience, of course, but, really, I want some proof of a go-getter mentality and ability to get things done. I would want to see proof that the students are able to earn. Same as comeback city angel investors.

Because investors and supporters push harder for something "real," founders building startups in comeback cities more commonly feel the need to prove it before seeking investment. As an investor, if you come to one of the comeback cities, you are more likely to find a proven product, a company with real revenue generation.

84 Austrian, Ziona & Piazza, Merissa. 2014. "Barriers and Opportunities for Entrepreneurship in Older Industrial Regions". 215-243.

Dave Jakubowski co-founded a company called Ureeka, which seeks to democratize expertise to eliminate geographic constraints, gender bias, and racial bias as barriers to access. In his research on this geographic barrier and the outcomes of startups in what he refers to as "silver cities"—tier 2 cities including Baltimore, Buffalo, Detroit, Cleveland, and St. Louis—he noted that what characterizes a startup in these places compared to Silicon Valley is that very few companies in these places have zero revenue compared to Silicon Valley where that is the norm.

Techstars' Ted Serbinski, who operates out of Detroit, has pointed out a geographic region between five points: Chicago, Ann Arbor, Pittsburgh, Cincinnati, and Indianapolis. Within this pentagon are Cleveland, Columbus, Akron, Fort Wayne, and Dayton, meaning three comeback cities fall within this zone and many other towns and cities impacted by each of their economies. Within this area exists eight of the top twenty-five entrepreneurial colleges, six of the top twenty engineering schools, and fifteen percent of Fortune 500 companies. Serbinski described this region, saying, "This is arguably one of the most talented regions in America, churning out the most real, revenue generating businesses."

As Serbinski saw it, these types of cities don't have any of "these social networks that will 'figure it out later.' "[85]

Not only does this undoubtedly appeal to the pervasive realism in many of the comeback cities, but as an investor, what more could you want?

---

85   Austin, John. 2018. "The Rust Belt Needs Capital to Turn Talent and Innovation into Jobs". *Brookings*. https://www.brookings.edu/blog/the-avenue/2018/08/14/the-rust-belt-needs-capital-to-turn-talent-and-innovation-into-jobs/.

CHAPTER 16

EAGER FOR A WINNING CULTURE

The classically accepted etymology of the word "fan" is believed to have come from the term "fanatic." Others believe the term may also have origins in the word "fancy," as in "I fancy a cup of strong coffee first thing in the morning."

The distinction between the two is important.

Liking a cup of coffee in the morning is a far cry from being a coffee fanatic. When you think of comeback city citizens, the latter is far more accurate when it comes to describing their feeling toward their cities and everything that represents them, including their sports teams and, hopefully, their start-ups and entrepreneurs in the future.

Let's stick with the sports fan analogy for a moment. Having grown up a faithful Buffalo Bills fan forced to witness pure domination of my team by the New England Patriots for twenty-plus years, I recoil every time I hear someone refer to the "Patriot Way," the essence cultivated in New England over their dynastic run. It's often accepted as fact that the culture head coach Bill Belichick has built has been the pre-eminent factor in the Patriots' success. But every once in a while, someone will bother to debate this, wondering whether having a good culture leads to winning or whether winning will lead to a good culture regardless. I tend to agree with the latter, and think that this concept holds especially true for entrepreneurship culture in comeback cities.

For entrepreneurship to be the fuel for long-term redevelopment in comeback cities, momentum is key.

Success begets success.

A rising tide raises all ships.

You can't be what you can't see.

You get the point. New and repeat entrepreneurs need to see others succeed in their area to help them see what is possible. Not only do successful companies serve as beacons of hope, but their founders and leaders are able to take on a mentorship role that is so important for the broader entrepreneurial community.

***

Steve Case echoes these sentiments of success begetting success:

> As you see more entrepreneurs with success [in cities outside of New York City, Silicon Valley, and Boston], that will lead to more capital flowing to these cities. As there's more capital flowing to these cities, more talent will stay there or move back there, that in turn will create a network effect increasing returns, which drives more capital, which drives more talent, which drives more ideas, which drives more startups, which drives more momentum. This doesn't happen overnight.[86]

As mentioned in the introductory paragraphs of this book, the city of Indianapolis is one that came up repeatedly throughout the research and writing process. In many cases, it was a positive example for many of the comeback cities I have chosen to focus on. A prime example of a successful startup story that could give rise to others around it is that of ExactTarget. ExactTarget is a Software as a Service (SaaS) company providing email marketing software applications and was started in 2000 with a $200,000 initial investment. With approximately 1,800 employees at its highest,

---

86 "AOL Founder Steve Case". 2019. Podcast. *Twenty Minute VC.*

ExactTarget was a homegrown Indianapolis success story. In 2013, they were acquired by SaaS behemoth Salesforce for $2.5 billion, adopting the name "Salesforce Marketing Cloud" in 2014.[87,88]

Aside from the optimism and shining star example Exact-Target provided for other Indianapolis entrepreneurs, their successful exit via acquisition by Salesforce has led to further investment in the area itself. Rather than hightail it to the West Coast, ExactTarget's operations remained in Indianapolis; furthermore, Salesforce as a whole has since invested in Indianapolis, establishing the city as its unofficial second headquarters. Salesforce occupies the tallest building in Indianapolis—Salesforce Tower—and has announced plans to hire more than 800 people in Indianapolis in the next two years and invest $40 million over the next ten. ExactTarget's co-founder and former CEO, Scott Dorsey, has taken steps to further advance the entrepreneurial community and economic development of Indianapolis, starting a venture fund and startup studio and joining a growing community

87 Engel, Jeff. "Scott Dorsey Reflects on ExacTtarget & the Rise of Indianapolis Tech". 2016. *Xconomy*. https://xconomy.com/indiana/2016/06/29/scott-dorsey-reflects-on-exacttarget-the-rise-of-indianapolis-tech/.

88 Upbin, Bruce. "Salesforce to Buy ExactTarget for $2.5 Billion". 2013. *Forbes*. https://www.forbes.com/sites/bruceupbin/2013/06/04/salesforce-to-buy-exacttarget-for-2-5-billion/#77a79e84cfcc.

of successful entrepreneurs to continue investing in the community that they have begun to see revitalize.[89,90]

In that same vein, Pittsburgh is a prime example of a comeback city that has developed a culture in conjunction with a few big wins. If you were to ask an out-of-towner what new industry niche Pittsburgh has carved out as of late, they would mention robotics and artificial intelligence, undoubtedly bringing up Uber's autonomous vehicle development in Pittsburgh. Although not a homegrown startup, Uber's investment in Pittsburgh has given it a certain attitude and legitimacy as an entrepreneurial force.

A natively built success story that gave Pittsburgh another niche upon which to build, though, is that of DuoLingo, which has led to further educational technology (edtech) successes. DuoLingo is a platform through which anyone—and I mean anyone—can learn a second language. Luis von Ahn, a Ph.D. alumnus from Carnegie Mellon University, co-founded and serves as CEO for the language-learning platform, and

---

89 Hensel, Anna. 2018. "How Salesforce's Acquisition of ExactTarget Helped Indianapolis' Tech Community Flourish". *Venturebeat.* https://venturebeat.com/2018/07/01/how-salesforces-acquisition-of-exacttarget-helped-indianapolis-tech-community-flourish/.

90 Briggs, James. "Salesforce reorganization to shed workers in Indianapolis". 2018. *Indianapolis Star.* https://www.indystar.com/story/money/2018/08/06/salesforce-reorganization-shed-workers-indianapolis/914544002/.

chose to keep its headquarters in Pittsburgh's up-and-coming East Liberty neighborhood. DuoLingo offers language learning courses to over 300 million users worldwide, and was most recently valued at $700 million.[91] The impressive growth of this company saw rise to other language technology companies such as Jibbigo (acquired by Facebook in 2013) and Carnegie Speech (raised over $11 million in funding).[92,93] All three companies have contributed tremendously in terms of job creation, economic impact, and reputation.

Without the success of DuoLingo, the road for other edtech and language processing companies in Pittsburgh would have been at the very least slightly more uphill. Alongside the success reaped by homegrown DuoLingo, Pittsburgh has furthered its legitimacy and winning culture as a startup hub through successful acquisitions of local companies that have increased the presence of giants like IBM, Microsoft, and Google.

While the reinvestment of successful entrepreneurs into their industries of expertise within their home cities, like

91 "DuoLingo". *Crunchbase.* https://www.crunchbase.com/organization/duolingo

92 Constine, Josh. "Facebook Acquires 'Mobile Technologies', Developer of Speech Translation App Jibbigo". 2013. *Techcrunch.* https://techcrunch.com/2013/08/12/facebook-acquires-mobile-technologies-speech-recognition-and-jibbigo-app-developer/.

93 "Carnegie Speech". *Crunchbase.* https://www.crunchbase.com/organization/carnegie-speech

Indianapolis and Pittsburgh, is likely more of a smart business move than it is one of benevolence, its effects on the local economy can be a positive externality because of the fanaticism of these cities' residents.

* * *

Buffalo, a city that would be considered a few steps behind Pittsburgh in the startup-driven redevelopment process, has its sights on its first big winner. ACV Auctions is likely to go public in the next couple of years and could be the culture setter that DuoLingo was in Pittsburgh, having brought more than 300 jobs to Buffalo as of summer 2019. ACV is a company whose app empowers car dealers to buy and sell used cars online instead of the traditional, cumbersome process of selling trade-in vehicles to used car dealers at one of the country's 300 physical used car auctions.

A feature in the Buffalo News described the company:

> *ACV is a tech company only the Rust Belt could produce. This is not, in other words, a cool or sexy product; Silicon Valley has not vied to improve the lives of the people ACV cofounder Joe Neiman calls "crusty old" car dealers. Neiman and his cofounder, Dan Magnuszewski, remember early meetings with coastal investors who grappled with the very concept of a used car. "Doesn't everyone buy new*

cars?" they'd ask, bewildered. Or: "Don't you think all cars will soon drive themselves?"

No longer the unlikely up-and-comer, a company like ACV has the opportunity to jettison Buffalo's relatively nascent startup ecosystem into a higher tier.[94]

When venture capital-backed startups get acquired or go public (as it is anticipated ACV Auctions will), there are anywhere from a few to a few dozen new millionaires created. The founders and co-founders will all have a significant cash out, but so too will many of the company's early employees. This cast of newly wealthy individuals will include some that will go fulfill their "retire on a yacht fantasies," but more likely the majority of them will start new companies, invest, or find philanthropic endeavors in the city that made them.

There are countless instances of startup communities to point to that have hit a lull, or perhaps are still working to get started. Despite having the right culture within many of these communities—individuals committed to their city and their cause—there are varying degrees of development and broader community advancement for any number of reasons.

---

94 Dewey, Caitlin. 2019. "Could This Be Buffalo's First Tech Goliath?". *The Buffalo News*. https://buffalonews.com/2019/05/10/acv-auctions-buffalo-from-the-bottom-to-1b-how-an-unsexy-startup-is-thriving-in-buffalo/.

But one of the quickest ways to accelerate that upswing is to find a success story to get behind.

Like a football team with a great locker room of individuals, their culture cannot make up for not having the talent and the pieces in place to win games. If a team with skilled players at all the necessary positions gets on a roll with a few wins under its belt, though, expect the culture to follow. Once culture meets talent, you truly have the opportunity for a dynasty to arrive, or in the case of these cities, a full-fledged comeback.

For comeback cities, a few big wins will go considerably farther for regional growth because of the huge impact it can have on each city's culture.

CHAPTER 17

LIMITED OPTIONS THEN, UNLIMITED POTENTIAL NOW

"It was either the Steel Mill or the Military." That's it. In my dad's mind there were only two options.

It was 1969 and my dad Al Gordon had just graduated high school. The country was at once marked with both an unbridled sense of freedom leftover from the past decade and a looming sense of unease. The Vietnam War had raged on beyond most expectations and the country was facing a draft lottery and more frequent and massive anti-war protests than had ever been seen. After a childhood and adolescence at Buffalo parochial schools, it was time to figure out his future so, naturally, he looked to those around him for options.

The seventh of eleven children, his mother was a homemaker and his father a steelworker at the Bethlehem Steel plant, along with 22,000 other steelworkers of this era.[95] Since the early 1900s when it had opened, the steel plant was booming as Buffalo's canals allowed it to be a hub for shipping its products throughout the Great Lakes. It was the most secure option any young Buffalonian could pursue. Of his three older brothers, all of them had joined the military. When he looked around to other friends and family in Lackawanna, NY where the steel plant was located just outside of Buffalo, it was pretty much the same story.

It was as simple as only having two options. It wasn't even that the steelworker life necessarily didn't appeal to my dad, but his brothers had gone into the military so that's what he would do too. He enlisted in the Army and went to Vietnam at age eighteen.

Upon returning home, he found his way to a rotational employment program for veterans with a local highway department. How did he come across this? Well, his brother Eugene had come back from war and found his way there. Because this program had no guaranteed funding beyond each month-at-hand, my dad was always looking for something else. In the help wanted ads, he found his way to a

95 Chavez, Lydia. "Bethlehem Steel to Cut 7,300 Jobs at Upstate Plant". 1982. *New York Times*. https://www.nytimes.com/1982/12/28/business/bethlehem-steel-to-cut-7300-jobs-at-upstate-plant.html.

printing company looking for a pressman and found out that you could make a decent living doing this, compared to the uncertainty of the highway department at that time. He ended up spending the next 40 years operating printing presses for various printing companies in and around Buffalo. Uncle Eugene stuck with the highway department for the rest of his four-plus decade career too.

* * *

When speaking with friends and acquaintances in cities such as Buffalo, Cleveland, Pittsburgh, or Baltimore, the same idea of limited, or unknown options continued to arise. In these cities that relied so heavily on one or two industries over the past half dozen generations, stability was revered and encouraged by parents and grandparents above all else for many younger individuals seeking life wisdom. People in these cities were generally humble, eager to work for a fair wage and the promise of relative security. With these principles and only a couple large, stable employers or industries in each city, it is easy to see why options seemed limited.

In a lot of ways, there didn't *need* to be a lot of options. These few employers could sustain the growing populations, who would promise them long, hard, consistent work. In exchange, workers received stability and generous benefits for the time.

For instance, beginning in the 1940s Cleveland's workforce was one of the most unionized in the nation and, as a result, they maintained one of the highest standards of living of any global industrial city. These included their high wages, along with:

> *Medical care and other fringe benefits provided through Blue Cross and other agencies encouraged by post-World War II federal legislation and supplemented after 1966 by the Federal Medicare system[,] retirement plans supplemented by the increasingly generous federal Social Security system, as well as by access for increasing numbers of their children to the expanding Cuyahoga Community College, Cleveland State University, and other state institutions of higher education whose tuitions were kept low through heavy tax subsidies.*[96]

Additionally, the large corporations took it upon themselves to take care of the city as a whole, from providing civic leadership to drawing national attention to driving local philanthropy. The relationship was symbiotic and agreeable, but it was too dependent upon continued industrial stability to be sustainable.

---

96 "Economy". 2018. *Encyclopedia of Cleveland History - Case Western Reserve University.* https://case.edu/ech/articles/e/economy.

Those who eventually recognized the need to make a shift often needed to go elsewhere to a larger city to improve their odds of success, particularly as the manufacturing industries of these cities truly started to wane in the latter half of the twentieth century. When we examine these cities from an entrepreneurial lens, the psychological state of risk aversion and thus self-limiting options is a clear barrier to developing a burgeoning startup ecosystem. While there are undoubtedly advantages to the characteristics of these cities' population (humble, gritty, resilient), getting current and future generations to shed the lingering idea of limited options is key. Especially because the future defining industries of these cities are yet to be fully determined, the menu of options for bright and ambitious people should not be expanded; it should be eliminated altogether.

Instead of viewing their life and career path as a choice between limited options, they should feel as though they have all the options in the world because, if their path doesn't already exist, they can build it from scratch.

You might be wondering why this culture of limited options that persists in many ways even today is a cultural trait that can be considered a positive for the future of comeback cities. The perspective here is a simple one. These cities have seen varying degrees of progress toward a renaissance despite fighting a culture of limited options.

The entrepreneurial baseline for comeback city citizens has been near zero for decades during which a large portion of the population didn't see this as an option. As more individuals embrace entrepreneurialism and choose to wipe away any previously limited menu of career options in favor of whatever they want to create, each city's renaissance will accelerate dramatically.

There is so much entrepreneurial potential waiting to be untapped.

PART 4

IGNITING THE COMEBACK: BREAK UP THE PAST TO SPARK THE FUTURE

"A society grows great when old men plant trees whose shade they know they shall never sit in."

—*GREEK PROVERB*

* * *

Recognizing the characteristics of comeback cities that make them well equipped to see a surge of entrepreneurialism en route to a resurgence is important to help others see what these cities' residents have known for so long. But talking about the traits is an empty exercise if there is no intention to take advantage of them.

I think of building a startup ecosystem in the same way I think about rebuilding a sports franchise. It is a blend of many of the same elements.

You need to bring in new faces to attract and maintain talent—owners, scouts, and coaches.

You need to incentivize good players to play for you while developing internally through amateur scouting and drafts.

You need to recognize the strengths of players already in your program.

You need to take a long-term approach in which you develop the right mix of young and old, rather than trying to go for the championship in year one and risk mortgaging your future.

You need to develop based on the day's current trends in the game (think training, analytics, etc.), while recognizing that these trends are ever-changing, requiring one eye to always be wandering ahead to keep you at the forefront of new innovations.

At the same time, the team will go nowhere if you rebuild and forget the past, leaving behind the fans and supporters that have been with you through the darkest of times. While they should not dictate the direction of the team, their continued buy-in is crucial to future success.

For cities seeking to retool and reinvent themselves through startups, the bottom line to reach their potential is a culture that embraces and exudes many of the traits described in what could be a successful rebuilding sports franchise. These traits are similar to the entrepreneurial spirit—centered around trying new things, failing, learning, trying again, and most importantly, never relenting. To engrain these ideas into comeback city culture, it needs to be done within the existing culture of each city.

To think that a new culture could be created entirely from scratch is not only unrealistic, it would be blasphemous to many of those who helped shape the existing culture of their comeback city. Instead, community leaders and entrepreneurial individuals must use the past to rethink the future, and not be afraid to think big and think long in doing so. To do so, let's lay out some tangible steps that should be taken.

Actions to be taken by comeback cities to ignite their respective comeback include:

1. Feed on nostalgia—make use of the yearning for the glory days that exists in comeback cities by reusing familiar spaces and ideas reminiscent of those days.

2. Take the long view—know that homegrown resurgence will take a long time, and every decision made should be done with a long-term, sustainable comeback in mind.

3. Engage the ecosystem—the startup ecosystem has many rings of involvement—from founders all the way to those who are only mildly aware of startup happenings—all must be brought along for the comeback to maximize success.

4. Start young—in the same vein of taking a long-term view, starting to promote entrepreneurialism and the tenets of a startup community among comeback city youth is key.

5. Incentivize risk-taking—comeback cities throughout their former prominence were sucked of a need to take risks, but this mind-set must be turned around to thrive around startups.

6. Explore different models—these cities need to think outside the box, refrain from planning and comparing based on places like Silicon Valley, and not be afraid of trying new models of startup-driven development.

CHAPTER 18

FEED ON NOSTALGIA

———

In a 2015 TED Talk at the University of Notre Dame, South Bend, IN mayor Pete Buttigieg poses the question, "What if a city has to rethink its past to understand its future?"

He begins his foray into this topic by introducing the story of the South Bend Watch Co. In 1909, South Bend was so well known for its innovation, engineering, and production, that one of the more famous watch companies of that time was named after the town itself. The pocket watches forged by the South Bend Watch Co. were considered best-in-class quality.

So, what happened? Why do we no longer recognize this brand at all, let alone as a best-in-class watch?

During World War 1, trench watches were widely used in favor of pocket watches because pocket watches were inconvenient for use in combat zones. The trench watch was the first step towards what we consider a wristwatch today. The South Bend Watch Co., instead of beginning to make trench watches, continued to make some of the best pocket watches in the world. By the 1930s, the company was out of business.

The lesson delivered in this story is not only the need to innovate to survive, but also the importance of refashioning what you already have to find its value into the future.[97] There are valuable cues for comeback cities to take from this example.

* * *

One of the side effects of past glory is a tendency of many comeback cities to live in the past. Buffalo and St. Louis both were host to world's fair in the twentieth century and have since become the punchline to too many jokes about their current economic state. A 2019 article about the Buffalo Bills football team having difficulty attracting big name free agents admitted "Buffalo is wielded like a Siberian threat." Former Bills general manager Buddy Nix said, "There's coaches that would say to free agents or guys that wasn't performing well, 'You better get your ass on the ball, or we're going to send you to Buffalo.' "[98]

---

97 Buttigieg, Pete. 2015. "What If a City Has to Rethink Its Past To Understand Its Future?". Video. *TEDxUND*.

98 Graham, Tim. 2019. "'Siberian' Stigma: How the Bills Recruit Free Agents To...". *The Athletic*. https://theathletic.com/790400/2019/01/29/

Other comeback cities face similar unoriginal insults.

With jabs like this thrown around regularly, it's easy to understand why proud residents would prefer to remind themselves of days when their city stood as a shining example of manufacturing, culture, innovation, and urban vibrancy instead. Because the visible marks of progress and success stories have been few and far between for these cities over the past half-century, successes gone by are held onto tightly. As a part of each city finding its own niche upon which to build its future, it must recognize the resources it has available, many that were developed as a part of its former glory.

These cities are reminded on a daily basis of past splendor in the former of faded, vacant architectural masterpieces and overgrown industrial parks. In a strange way, these apparitions serve not only as a sad reminder of the past, but also as a reminder of the potential each of these cities had.

This feeling of nostalgia is not to be ignored.

* * *

Compared to newer cities with little former prominence, these cities have a past to take pride in. To build a brand-new

---

siberian-stigma-how-the-bills-recruit-free-agents-to-buffalo-and-why-deep-pockets-dont-always-help/.

workspace to house a city's burgeoning startups would be undoubtedly met with fanfare amongst those in the entrepreneurial community. However, if that same space was set upon a foundation built during that city's pinnacle decades, the community beyond its entrepreneurial core would be abuzz.

Let's take a look at Detroit, for example. Built in the city's Corktown neighborhood in 1913 and dedicated the following year, the Michigan Central station was the tallest train station in the world and housed thousands of workers in the thirteen-story office tower above the rail depot. Beginning around World War I, hundreds of trains would leave the station each day and it became a hub of transportation for the thriving Midwest. Designed by the same architects who completed New York's Grand Central Station, the Michigan Central station was a towering representation of Detroit's esteem, constructed in the Beaux Arts style recognized by its ornate and detailed features. After rail travel began to decline after World War II, the station's prominence began to fade until it closed its operations in 1988. Since then, it has been the object of numerous would-be development projects that never came to fruition.[99]

---

99 Burton, Cindy. "Ford says it will spend $740M to bring Detroit train station project to life". *Detroit Free Press.* https://www.freep.com/story/money/business/2018/08/15/michigan-central-station-corktown-cost-740-million/994867002/

As each year passed, the station began to wane along with the city itself nearby. Forgotten architectural wonders like this gave rise to the genre called ruins photography, of which Detroit became the unofficial epicenter because of the widespread abandonment of buildings and structures. In an essay on the past and future of this structure, Detroit-born journalist, Tamara Warren, described the station:

> *For decades, the dilapidated presence of the once majestic train station stung residents as an ominous reminder of widespread neglect. The 18-story building towers over Michigan Avenue, and while it made for a lucrative set piece on the film Batman v Superman, it represents a deep, complex wound. It is a physical reminder of what the city was, and what it many thought it would never be again. It's a punchline, a romanticized and ruined tourist destination [...] but all that may soon change.*[100]

We've talked about its new niche in mobility, having found what will hopefully be one of its economic drivers for years to come. Building upon this newfound hope, Ford Motor Company bought the station in 2018. Around 2,500 employees, most of whom work on mobility projects, will work in

---

100 Warren, Tamara. "Inside Detroit's Crumbling Train Station That Ford Plans to Transform into a Mobility Lab". 2018. *The Verge*. https://www.theverge.com/2018/6/20/17483696/ ford-detroit-train-station.

this refurbished space intended to be an innovation hub for Ford and autonomous vehicle development.[101]

Another Detroit-based company that made use of nostalgia to drive interest in its brand is watchmaker Shinola. The name itself was purchased from an early 1900s shoe polish company, and they market all products with a nostalgic and Detroit-based theme. They use the historic Argonaut building, once known as the General Motors Research Laboratory as a headquarters, watch factory, and bicycle workshop. The quality-made association with the Detroit of yesteryear has led to considerable success and growth for Shinola, along with hundreds of jobs created and kept in the city of Detroit.[102]

Buffalo has a similarly well-known ruin that anyone approaching downtown will pass on their drive in. A cascade of abandoned grain elevators sits along Lake Erie that have been known as a destination for photographers, vandals, urban explorers, and not much else for decades. In 2014, local business owner Rick Smith purchased several of the elevators in what is known as Silo City. Smith hopes these relics of years gone by can become a place where culture and commerce intersect. Thus far, their Silo City is home to

---

101 Ibid

102 "Imported from Detroit: Shinola Settles into Taubman Center". 2012. *Curbed Detroit*. https://detroit.curbed.com/2012/8/7/10343488/imported-from-detroit-shinola-introduces-neomanufacturing-to-detroit#more.

a performing arts center, historic tours, art workshops, and private events, with further development still to come. Even without becoming the home of new business drivers like Detroit's train depot makeover, Silo City has equally stirred the Buffalo community because it is a familiar face getting a much-needed makeover.

Taking advantage of the nostalgia on which cities such as Detroit and Buffalo thrive is vital to getting the broader community on board. Ford's plans for the Michigan Central station are widely known across the Detroit metropolitan region, and the widespread enthusiasm will undoubtedly have broader implications for the city's development and entrepreneurial spirit.

As Buttigieg summed it up, "You have to make it new but you don't have to make it up."

CHAPTER 19

TAKE THE LONG VIEW

———

A necessary mind-set that must be adopted by comeback city residents who believe in the force of entrepreneurship in reinvigorating their city is one that they are uniquely evolved to adopt. This mind-set of steadfastness in the face of slow progress is imperative when looking at a region's homegrown development. The love of place and optimism that a resurgence will ultimately come, as discussed in prior chapters, is evidence of this steadfastness.

As such, comeback cities are psychologically evolved to handle the needed long-term vision that must be developed for sustainable entrepreneurial growth. With their "not too big, not too small" sizing, these cities are also uniquely equipped to create a shared extended view of where they will be long down the road.

In the same vein, one of Brad Feld's principles of a vibrant startup community is a long-term commitment because "economies grow, peak, decline, bottom out, grow again, peak again, decline again, and bottom out again. Some of these cycles are modest. Some are severe. The lengths vary dramatically."[103]

Referring to the various elements of the entrepreneurial ecosystem, Feld expands, "Universities function in a one-year time horizon and I like to joke that they have summer off. The government functions in two-to-four year rhythms with an election year. So, they're functioning for one-to-three years, not 20. Big business has a quarterly, annual rhythm. So, you have to be able to transcend all the ups and downs in the shorter-term measurement when you're building the startup community."[104] Comeback cities must look beyond the few years' timeline that these cycles could entail.

In Detroit, an innovator working in artificial intelligence in the autonomous vehicle arena told me his concerns about taking a short-term vision. The entrepreneurial community must create a vision rather than policymakers, city, and state

103 Feld, Brad, and David Kaplan. 2012. *Startup Communities: Building an Entrepreneurial Ecosystem in Your City.* Hoboken, NJ: John Wiley and Sons, Inc.

104 "Techstars' Brad Feld: A Startup Community Needs a 20-Year Time Horizon". 2013. Podcast. *Knowledge@Wharton.* https://knowledge.wharton.upenn.edu/article/techstars-brad-feld-a-startup-community-needs-a-20-year-time-horizon/.

leaders because political terms are limiting. A two-, four-, or eight-year political term is not long enough to create a sustained change. Even if a magic bullet short-term incentive brought multiple massive companies to Detroit, the city's infrastructure could not support this change. This is part of the reason the growing affluent tech employees of Detroit are generally living *outside* of the city itself. This is not the grand urban comeback we are envisioning.

Currently, there is not enough talent in the city to support a massive boom in highly-skilled employment. Even if they were able to equally incentivize relocation to Detroit for new talent, the city's housing and school systems would not be adequate to support the influx. Anyone who lives in Detroit would tell you it is ludicrous to think that injecting a few new companies into the city is going to fix any of its underlying woes—widespread inequality, child poverty rates at nearly fifty percent,[105] and forty percent of households with no access to the internet.[106] Taking the long-term approach to address underlying and infrastructural issues is the only way to ensure any kind of entrepreneurial growth is sustained.

---

105 MacDonald, Christine. "Detroiters' income rises for second year but poverty rate doesn't improve". 2018. *The Detroit News*. https://www.detroitnews.com/story/news/local/detroit-city/2018/09/13/census-detroiters-income-rise/1268641002/.

106 Hudson, Marc. "Detroit's Broadband Infrastructure". 2015. *FCC*. http://transition.fcc.gov/c2h/10282015/marc-hudson-presentation-10282015.pdf

* * *

Additionally, in a city like Detroit where the region's new niche of mobility and autonomous vehicles is a relatively new industry from a global perspective, it is key to take the long approach to sustaining that leg up as the industry leader. In an industry that could ultimately replace the two million truckers with self-driving alternatives, it is imperative that those paving the path forward consider the complications that will come in their desired future state. For instance, as those in Detroit driving progress on autonomous vehicles are working to make the necessary advancements, they too should be considering the fallout and pushback of their work so as to maximize their long-term viability.

In a shift toward automation that could have effects reminiscent of the departure of so many manufacturing jobs that once defined comeback cities, Detroit leaders whose niche industry will play an active role in displacing one of America's largest employment categories should actively play a role in helping mitigate the negative impact. Despite the likely positive macroeconomic impact of the automation shift, there will be considerable microeconomic impacts for the regions and cities most affected. Motor vehicle operator jobs will begin to disappear. Supply chains and logistics will be redefined. Taking the long-term vision to see things like this will allow for the possibility of a sustainably built industry for comeback cities.[107]

"Take a long-term vision." Easier said than done, right? Sounds like a job for policymakers, no?

The entrepreneurial ecosystem has a huge role to play.

To reinvent these cities and rely on state and local incentives, policies, and dollars to do the trick would be to repeat history's mistakes. Each piece of the entrepreneurial puzzle—from founders to investors to everyone in between—must take a long-term view as well. Seeking solutions with double- and triple-bottom lines (meaning those that are good from a financial, social, and environmental standpoint all at the same time), sharing their experience and talents with the community openly, taking an extra step to promote inclusion whenever possible, and making use of unconventional partnerships to address underlying community issues will be key.

The culture of comeback cities makes them places that can breed entrepreneurs that feel a sense of community accountability. This will be a sticking point in the argument that

---

107 Rushe, Dominic. 2017. "End of the Road: Will Automation Put an End To the American Trucker?". *The Guardian*. https://www.theguardian.com/technology/2017/oct/10/american-trucker-automation-jobs.

these places are uniquely equipped to enact a long-term vision.

Where the community goes, so too will individual startups. And where individual startups go, so too will the community.

CHAPTER 20

ENGAGE THE ECOSYSTEM

When some people hear "ecosystem" while talking about pretty much anything besides the interconnected organisms that make up a rainforest, they roll their eyes. Find a better word for the interconnected organisms that make up a community's startup scene, and you have my permission to roll those eyes as far back as they'll go. When referring to a startup community and its many players as an ecosystem, we are reemphasizing the importance of taking a comprehensive approach. An approach that recognizes the varying levels of actors, their needs, and their relationships. An ecosystem approach is the only way that any startup-driven economic development will ever take shape.

For an entrepreneurial ecosystem, taking a step back to see all the pieces is crucial because the entire city and region need to feel a part of the development for it to mean anything. One qualitative measure of performance is what I like to refer to as the dad test. Would a stereotypical dad—or at least my dad—or someone who loves to talk about the good old days and is generally not thrilled with drastic change (sorry, pops):

A) notice any entrepreneurial growth in his area, and

B) take any noticeable growth as a sign that things are actually turning around at a bigger level than a new company opening down the road?

When the answer to both questions is yes, congratulations. Your startup ecosystem has matured to the point that even the most peripheral organisms are involved. To pass the dad test, there are countless groups and institutions that must be brought along for the entrepreneurial rise of a community.

An EY thought piece on the five elements of a startup ecosystem examines this ecosystem through the lens of one of our comeback cities: Cincinnati. In the past five to ten years, Cincinnati has felt momentum for its entrepreneurial revival, during which local organizations united to spur the city's tech-based economy. All of these pieces took over a decade to develop individually, while working collaboratively toward a city-wide mission.

The "power five" elements in play in any entrepreneurial ecosystem are some combination of:

1. Startups
2. Investors
3. Institutions
4. Governments
5. Corporations

Per EY's thought piece:

> *Although the needs of these entities vary, each requires access to the other and, consequently, ecosystem stakeholders are increasingly interdependent. For instance, customers for start-ups can be corporations, educational institutions or governments. Corporations can access innovation through direct interactions with start-ups, or through introductions via other corporations, investors, educational institutions and the government. These complex, crisscrossed relationships demand each of the five to think and behave as a maximalist contributing its share while joining forces, so when success is achieved, each of the ecosystem partners wins.*

* * *

In Cincinnati, corporations served the role of ignitor. Ten Fortune 500 companies call the region home, including Procter & Gamble and Kroger, whose participation was key in the Cincinnati Business Committee's push to establish

Cintrifuse. Cintrifuse, as described in a previous chapter, provides the mentorship and partnership between new companies and existing behemoths. It also allows for a space in which the remaining components of the Cincinnati entrepreneurial ecosystem can link up. One of the other unique contributions of Cintrifuse to the community is hosting its signature annual event Innovation Xchange, during which startups and large companies can share knowledge, resources, and ideas. To take advantage of its place as "one of the top branding, marketing and design hubs of the US [...] home to consumer products and retail giants such as Procter & Gamble, Kroger, Macy's and 84.51°," Cincinnati also created the Brandery, which was meant to connect startups with world-class marketing agencies around the world.[108]

From the Cincinnati big corporations' perspective, this was not a wholly benevolent effort. There was something in it for them too. But the beauty of their role in the startup ecosystem is that their success and startups' success are not mutually exclusive; on the contrary, by playing the role of ignitor, these corporations ultimately benefited in three ways as well:

---

108 Fang, Sara. "Accelerating Start-Up Ecosystems with the Power of 5". 2015. *EY Consulting.* https://consulting.ey.com/accelerating-start-up-ecosystems-with-the-%e2%80%9cpower-of-5%e2%80%9d/.

1. As very large publicly-traded companies, they were under pressure to deliver organic growth and internal efficiency through digital talent and innovation. Startup partnerships offered them an avenue to this exact goal.
2. New and innovative talent could be attracted to the area by a vibrant startup ecosystem, a talent pool that would contribute as talent to these big corporations in the long run as well.
3. Efforts in traditional economic development for the region were not paying off fast enough for the big corporations' liking. These efforts were expensive, relied too heavily on incentives, and weren't providing the local economy in which these big corporations wanted to play.

Cincinnati's cross-state comeback city neighbor, Cleveland, has a significant opportunity to improve its ecosystem by engaging institutions that it has not yet taken full advantage of. According to an assessment of its ecosystem, Cleveland has limited engagement with the city's governmental organizations, and so the current approach from these bodies is a traditional top-down approach to entrepreneurship. Similarly, there appear to be limited relationships between the startup network and existing corporations beyond local accelerator Plug and Play's relationship with the Cleveland Clinic. In not fostering these relationships, startups in Cleveland are missing out on mentorship, innovation programs, investments, and research and development opportunities.

To capture its full potential, Cleveland must work on engaging all of these players in a cohesive manner.[109]

Beyond the initial sphere of entrepreneurial ecosystem players, those with the power, drive, and commitment to forge a city's vision for the future should also consider the more peripheral organizations, groups, and individuals who will not only be affected by entrepreneurial activity, but who could play an active role given the right level of engagement. Each neighborhood within an aspiring entrepreneurial city and region should be engaged, particularly when their area will be impacted by new businesses or startup activities. Having a pulse on the political, social, and cultural landscape, and aligning your city-wide vision to these elements will ensure that as the city progresses for entrepreneurs and those directly involved, so too does it progress for its everyday citizens.

* * *

Beyond the players both directly and indirectly involved in the ecosystem, an overarching part of the ecosystem that must be focused on is density and access to expertise. Part of the rationale for Dave Jakubowski in starting the previously mentioned company Ureeka (seeking to democratize

---

109 "Assessment & Roadmap Report: Cleveland, OH". 2018. *Techstars Startup Community Development Program.*

expertise to eliminate geographic, gender, and racial biases)
comes from research showing differences in access to expertise in primary markets versus others. Research showed that
the rate of company generation was generally higher in places
like comeback cities compared to the major tech corridors
in New York and the Bay Area. However, it costs an average
of $250,000 more per year to get a company off the ground
in these secondary markets.

The reason behind this gap in expenses is related to access
to expertise. According to Jakubowski, "If somebody in San
Francisco wants to know what's the back door to get into
Instagram shopping, for instance, chances are they know
someone who works there or can have some networking
connect and get a free kick. That's very difficult to do in a
place like Cleveland."

Because specific needs for vendors and consultants like this
are frequent for young companies without dedicated teams
for many of the needs that arise, founders in areas like comeback cities spend far more money cycling through multiple
vendors and consultants, whereas founders in somewhere
like New York City can find the right person to help them
far more easily. As such, Ureeka seeks to make a network
of experts available to people in places that do not have
the luxury of just the right person for every need within
close proximity.

For comeback cities, making use of virtual networks like this, along with tapping into the expertise of people who might be comeback city natives, but have left to grow a career elsewhere, are methods to overcome this challenge. Pieces of the ecosystem do not have to be standing in front of you in person to be a huge contributor to collective growth.

With all the pieces working together, a city can rise around the startup ecosystem. Even to the point that dad might get in the mix.

CHAPTER 21

START YOUNG

A basic tool in problem solving and understanding the root cause of a challenge is called the "Five Whys Technique." This technique is naturally practiced by toddlers all over the world: look at the end result or current situation and ask "Why?" five times to uncover the underlying cause and it has become one of the principles of lean problem solving.[110]

A common illustration of this technique stems from Don Messersmith, entomology professor at the University of Maryland who spent the late 1980s and early 1990s studying the effects of midges and birds on the Lincoln and Jefferson Memorial Monuments in Washington, D.C. A midge is a bug, to be clear. During this time, the monuments were noted to be deteriorating, with marble "[eroding] so badly in spots that last year a chunk of one 42-foot column at the Jefferson

---

110 Serrat, Olivier. "The Five Whys Technique". *Knowledge Solutions.* Singapore: Springer.

Memorial crashed to the ground and other columns were found to be teetering dangerously."[111]

The main problem to be addressed, as illustrated by the falling column, was the deterioration of two of America's most famous monuments.

Why #1—Why is this deterioration occurring?

The consensus was that frequently cleaning with high-powered sprayers and chemicals were causing the immediate damage.

Why#2—Why was cleaning required so frequently?

As anyone who got close enough to the monuments could see, this was due to excessive bird droppings.

Why #3—Why are there so many birds flocking to these two locations?

Birds were attracted to these monuments because of the abundance of spiders found around them.

---

111 Angier, Natalie. "Debate on Buildings: To Scrub or Not". 2019. *New York Times.* https://www.nytimes.com/1992/01/14/science/debate-on-buildings-to-scrub-or-not.html.

Why #4—Why are there so many spiders?

Messersmith's research helped identify that midges—a type of insect—were food for spiders and there was an enormous midge population around these monuments.

Why #5—Why is the midge population so large?

Herein lies the root cause of the deterioration—midges are attracted to the lights that shine on the monuments at night. Addressing this root cause by reducing the amount of time lights shone on the monuments at night reduced the midges, which reduced the spiders, which reduced the bird dropping, which reduced the frequent cleaning, which reduced the deterioration.

* * *

When we look at the complex social, cultural, political, and economic circumstances that led to comeback cities' current situation, this technique is likely to oversimplify. In the same way that monument deterioration does not solely come down to cleaning (think of the effects of weather, aging, pollution, etc.), the cause and thus potential solution to comeback cities' current situation cannot be simplified to one thing.

But if you ask why enough times, you get past answers that led to the historic decline of industry and begin asking why much of the decline has persisted decades after the initial and abrupt economic changes occurred. Enough "whys" down the road and you will get to the point where the answer is that the youth of comeback cities are not, broadly speaking, brought up in a way that would encourage or incentivize them (from neither a parenting nor societal standpoint) to change the fortunes of their hometown en mass.

Starting to promote, encourage, and reward entrepreneurship at a young age is one of the most vital ways to create a sustained culture of building within these cities. Even those who have successful academic careers tend to leave town for college elsewhere. Once there, they are led to enter the corporate recruiting circuit. Instead, from a young age, people need to be encouraged to forge their own path. This should be celebrated, not judged.

Venture for America founder and author of *Smart People Should Build Things,* Andrew Yang, lays out his viewpoint of the trajectory of our most talented young people as it currently stands:

> *When I was younger, I subscribed to a general view of our educational system that goes something like this: If you study hard and do well in high school, you'll get into a*

good college. Where you go to college is very important. Then, if you do well in college, perhaps you'll go on to law school or med school, or maybe academia if you're an intellectual sort. In any case, if you're smart and work hard, you'll wind up with a good job.

That "good job," in this scenario, is a job that requires a lot of complex analytical thinking and pays well, like investment banking or management consulting[...] This is our system of training and employment, and it functions very well. Smart, hardworking kids go to good schools and get trained for good jobs. The job market operates with great efficiency, and that is a big reason why our economy is so successful.

There's another view of the current system, though: that it is a mess.

Ambitious college students have no real idea what to do upon graduation, but they're trained to seek the "next level." Many apply to law school, graduate school, or even medical school because of a vague notion of status and progress rather than a genuine desire or natural fit. Those who try to do something independently often find themselves frustrated by their lack of rapid advancement, and so default to a more structured path of law school, business school, or graduate school.

The concentration in professional services leads our national university graduates to congregate in a handful of metropolitan areas—primarily New York City, Silicon Valley, Boston, and Washington, DC. Those who become bankers or consultants are highly paid and heavily socialized, yet many become disaffected due to a lack of purpose an unsustainable lifestyle, and some simply discover they don't enjoy their roles. We train thousands more lawyers each year than legal jobs exist for, and hundreds more academics than there are academic jobs. Each path throws off waves of refugees who are often at a loss as to what to do with themselves, only at that point they're in their late twenties, possibly in debt or used to an expensive lifestyle, and trained to do something narrow and specific.

Meanwhile, massive needs in other sectors are not being met. American companies need smart people who can manage, operate, innovate, and improve them. And startups and early-stage growth companies are in desperate need of talent in order to create jobs and drive economic progress. The metropolitan areas of Detroit, New Orleans, Baltimore, Philadelphia, Cleveland, Cincinnati, and Las Vegas account for over $1 trillion of US gross domestic product and represent a vastly diverse range of industries. The trajectory of the young growth companies in these cities and others like them will determine the direction *of our economy. Detroit alone is our twelfth largest metro region, with over 3.6 million people. Its post-bankruptcy renewal is one of the great projects of this age. Unfortunately, it doesn't have a giant recruitment arm to make the case on college campuses.*

Our identification and distribution of talent in the United States has gone from being a historic strength to a critical weakness. We've let the market dictate what our smart kids do, and they're being systematically funneled into obvious, structured paths that don't serve them or the economy terribly well.[112]

* * *

This is not easy considering the risk averse tendencies of older generations within comeback cities (it is important to acknowledge that it is no *one's* fault that this is the case), but if the change occurs in youth, it will grow with each coming generation.

Urban planner, Akron, OH native, and Rust Belt advocate Jason Segedy talks about the reality of cultural risk aversion in older generations and notes the opportunity at hand in the youth of comeback cities:

---

112 Yang, Andrew. 2014. *Smart People Should Build Things*. New York, NY: HarperBusiness.

I feel some nostalgia for an era that I didn't really live through, and mostly don't remember, because it was still in the cultural DNA of my childhood. But then I think of my 47-year-old uncle getting killed in 1983, on the job at B.F. Goodrich, by a malfunctioning piece of machinery, and a lot of the romance immediately wears off.

Millennials are even more of a blank slate, as they have no living memory at all of that time. I find that most of them (again, I'm generalizing) lack the emotional baggage, and therefore much of the cynicism and bitterness of some older residents.[113]

Therein lies the opportunity.

Young people in comeback cities did not witness their downfall firsthand. They are capable of taking the positives from the culture in which they were raised—grittiness, pride, pragmatism—without the negatives. If comeback cities make a point to encourage and support these young people in being builders, they will be the architects of a revamped city that all generations can be proud of again.

---

113 Segedy, Jason. 2018. "Why are Some People in the Rust Belt So Resistant to Change?". *Cleveland Scene.* https://www.clevescene.com/scene-and-heard/archives/2018/12/07/why-are-some-people-in-the-rust-belt-so-resistant-to-change.

So, what can be done to instill in the youth a mind-set that many of their elders have not put at the cornerstone of their own careers? There are opportunities to enact programs like what Revolution Partner Mary Grove and State Commissioner of Employment and Economic Development Steve Grove have founded in Minnesota, a region that shares many traits of comeback cities. The organization, called Silicon North Stars, takes rising ninth graders from underserved communities in Minnesota and provides them the community and resources to pursue forward-looking technology careers through tech camps and ongoing programming to continue connections with the tech community.[114] The program's first rounds of Silicon North Stars have since moved on to success in colleges.[115]

This still is not easy. Ask anyone whose life mission is in this area. It's a slog. A worthwhile slog, but a slog nonetheless.

At an individual and family level, though, is where the broadest impact can be felt. In what many parents would find to be counterproductive to their instinct to protect their children at all costs, moms and dads must develop and encourage

114 "Overview". 2019. *Silicon North Stars Youth Program*. http://www.siliconnorthstars.org/overview/.

115 Kennedy, Patrick. "Nonprofit Plugs Twin Cities Teens into Silicon Valley Tech". 2018. *Star Tribune*. http://www.startribune.com/twin-cities-team-tackle-silicon-valley-during-tech-camp/490027101/.

traits that help their children become successful entrepreneurs. This includes taking risks and opening oneself up for failure as a method of furthering progress and development. It includes shunning paths that are often considered the safest or most secure. But most importantly, it includes embracing independence and accountability, and the ability to truly think big.

Alongside the notion of taking a long-term vision from a citywide perspective, it is important for parents to recognize the future needs of the market and how they are changing. It is important for parents to reconsider what they have traditionally thought to be "good" paths for their children.

Perhaps a bit harshly stated, but one comeback city entrepreneurship professor insists the best thing we can do for future generations is to "shut up" as advice givers when we think we know what path is best.

I would take it one step further: rather than shut up, we should be there to show up for the young people of tomorrow's comeback cities. Show up by walking the walk, giving first, embracing the community and its future. In doing so, it won't seem like such a crazy idea to the young people that will ultimately be charged with completing these comebacks.

CHAPTER 22

INCENTIVIZE RISK-TAKING

———

We live in a world where Instagram influencers and motivators churn out quotes about risk-taking as if each and every day they wake up, eat their Icelandic yogurt, and pause to think, "Today is the day I take that leap. Today is the day everything changes."

Let me just give you a taste of the posts that come up when you search #takerisks on Instagram:

"Comfort is the biggest enemy of your dreams."

"Let today be the day you give up who you've been, for who you became."

"In the end, we only regret the chances we didn't take."

And my personal favorite:

"While you're still acting scared to take a risk and feeling stuck...Burger King out here making tacos..."

Sometimes these types of inspirational quotes hit home. Most of the time, though, they just feel too lofty to take seriously.

When we talk about taking risks as an entrepreneur, you do not have to scare yourself half to death every day to be successful. It is about embracing the notion of failure as not only a possibility, but a probability. More importantly, it is another step towards success. A good startup ecosystem not only promotes this idea, but they live it through the safeguards they set up around their entrepreneurs.

Alongside changing the culture and mind-set about taking risks and "making stuff," comeback cities should identify ways to incentivize risk-taking for those that are in a position to do so. There are a number of ways to do so, and each city should consider its own best option.

One method of incentivizing risk-taking is by diminishing the magnitude of the risk to begin with. When I pause to think about the different fates of comeback cities compared to some cities you may expect to be grouped in (see the chapter titled, "Don't Be Mad Your City Didn't Make the Cut"), I go back to high school biography class in my mind. Please note I said high school so I cannot be held culpable for the scientific validity of every word that is about to follow, but the analogy is still relevant.

* * *

I am sure you may remember the rapid speciation of Darwin's finches, in which different species of finch appeared on various islands in the Galápagos archipelago, because each species adapted to have different types of beaks uniquely suited to the abundant food source on each island. For example, there was one kind of finch whose beak was long and skinny so that it could reach cactus flowers without its body being poked.

I am now realizing this is the third bird-related story in this book and it is taking all of my willpower to not retroactively retitle this book "From the Ashes: Startups in America's Phoenix Cities."

Sorry, back on track here.

Comeback cities were like the cactus finch in their degree of specialization. Whether it was steel, grain, or automobiles, these cities evolved to flourish based on their abundant resource for more than a century before, suddenly, that resource or industry disappeared. This is like some kind of invasive species wiping out the cacti on those finches' island.

They are so uniquely equipped to sustain themselves on these cacti that they quickly would become on the verge of extinction.

On the other hand, if finches on another island had beaks that had not evolved to such extremes, the wiping out of one source of food would not doom them. If the cacti disappear, perhaps their beaks are not so narrow that they can still use them to grab nuts, seeds, or insects and continue onward. Kansas City comes to mind as an example of a city who did not specialize to the extent of comeback cities and thus never experienced a downturn of that magnitude.

From a city-wide perspective, avoiding overspecialization will be paramount in avoiding the same mistakes of the past.

* * *

Looking at incentivizing the individual to take risks, solve problems, and start businesses, the predominant theory for incentivizing the risk involved in starting a company is that financial support is the most effective way to get companies off the ground. There are state and federal government options to pursue, including low interest loans, tax breaks, and grants for entrepreneurs to start businesses.

At the same time, ecosystemic things, such as talent pools, research and development landscapes, and others, are important for sustained growth as an entrepreneurial community. To get people to take that final step towards following their idea or burgeoning enterprise, there are also things such as seed funds, pitch competitions (which both include funding, access to investors, and support to shape/develop ideas with consultants/universities), free office space, connections to social networks and partnerships, and further training in specific areas to strengthen the business.

At the broader incentive level, some communities have created economic opportunity zones to bolster business by providing tax-free businesses for consumers. Globally, these have been referred to as free trade zones and have been attempted in conflict zones. A more commonly known variation of this are the Opportunity Zones created as part of the Tax Cuts and Jobs Act of 2017. These zones are meant to encourage long-term development in low-income urban and rural communities nationwide by providing significant tax incentives.

An example of a targeted tax incentive provided at the state level is a 2018 Maryland tax credit available to investors who specifically invest in cybersecurity ventures, an effort to build upon Baltimore's cyber success in recent years. "Maryland's cybersecurity sector is a hotbed of ideas, imagination and innovation, and investors are taking notice," according to

Maryland Commerce Secretary Mike Gill. "Offering an incentive to investors is a great way to attract even more capital to the entrepreneurs who are working to keep our nation safe and secure."[116]

In fine-tuning each comeback city's niche, it allows policymakers and other players to get on board and spur targeted development in this manner.

Some of the other techniques discussed—including starting to build entrepreneurial rewards systems for younger generations and building a winning culture—are more cultural effects to be pursued in tandem with these often policy-based incentive options.

* * *

Back to the concept of normalizing failure, this topic came up time and time again when talking to entrepreneurs across comeback cities. Depending on who I was chatting with, their exact wording was particular—anywhere from celebrating failure to normalizing failure to tolerating failure. In any case, the point was well-taken: that these cities are plagued by the

---

116 Babcock, Stephen. "Maryland Just Opened Up a Tax Credit for Cybersecurity Investors". 2018. *Technical. ly Baltimore.* https://technical.ly/baltimore/2018/09/13/ maryland-opens-up-tax-credit-for-cybersecurity-investors/.

notion that taking a leap of faith on yourself or your career and failing is a scarlet letter that you may not come back from.

To get people to be willing to take risks, the culture of the city needs to shift towards celebrating the attempt more so than ridiculing the failure. When speaking with investors specifically, not only did they accept founders with former failures, but it was a trait that they deemed as promising for a potential investment.

From both an entrepreneur perspective and a community development perspective, investing capital or resources into not just one company and calling it quits is likely to have a familiarly negative outcome. To get entrepreneurs and potential entrepreneurs comfortable with risk, they must know that failure is not a death sentence; there will be other opportunities and there is no element of shame. For leaders, investors, and supporters, putting your efforts into a multitude of companies, industries, and founders will hedge against the risk that could potentially dissuade you.

The cultural change to embrace risk is perhaps the most difficult to achieve, but its impact is the greatest.

CHAPTER 23

EXPLORE DIFFERENT MODELS

———

Remember the quote from Marc Andreessen in chapter 3, "The world would be much better if we had 50 more Silicon Valleys."?

I still agree, but it is important to recognize that not every community should strive to be Silicon Valley.

One of the myths about startup communities described in Techstars co-founder Brad Feld's book *Startup Communities: Building an Entrepreneurial Ecosystem in your City* is exactly this: that a good startup community needs to be like Silicon Valley. Journalist Neil Koenig describes some of the reasons Silicon Valley because what it is, showing us that replication is surely unlikely:

> *Silicon Valley has unique characteristics just like every city does, and every city and community should focus*

on their unique characteristics. They should learn from the things that have caused Silicon Valley to be such an extraordinary, entrepreneurial ecosystem. But they shouldn't try to emulate it. Silicon Valley has been developing as a startup community for over 60-70 years."[117] Among the factors that led to Silicon Valley's success are time and timing. Not only has it developed over six or more decades, but it benefited from cheap, abundant land after World War II with a major city nearby, along with a mass of startup successes in the midst of the internet boom.[118]

This myth that other cities can be like Silicon Valley was echoed by investors, entrepreneurs, and academics that I spoke to across all seven comeback cities, noting that relying on the rapid emergence of multiple unicorns—that is, a startup valued at over $1 billion—to pave the trail for a flourishing entrepreneurial city is not going to work in these cities. Besides the sheer amount of circumstances that would have to fall into place to replicate a community like Silicon Valley, many of the unique cultural and structural characteristics of the entrepreneurial ecosystems within comeback cities

---

117 "Techstars' Brad Feld: A Startup Community Needs a 20-Year Time Horizon". 2013. Podcast. *Knowledge@Wharton*. https://knowledge.wharton.upenn.edu/article/techstars-brad-feld-a-startup-community-needs-a-20-year-time-horizon/.

118 Koenig, Neil. "Secret of Silicon Valley's Success". 2014. *BBC News*. https://www.bbc.com/news/technology-26041341.

make them better suited for more organic growth. Don't get me wrong, unicorn success stories are important to draw the types of talent needed for a sustained startup community, but comeback cities should not rely solely on their emergence to build their own thriving entrepreneurial community.

* * *

Structural issues facing comeback cities may be the biggest impediment to replicating a Silicon Valley model. Although the amount of venture capital going to areas outside of New York City, Silicon Valley, and Massachusetts has gained more attention and progress from venture capital funds, there is still a considerable gap in growth stage venture funding. Across the board, comeback cities feel this gap is near the top of the most crucial improvement areas for their particular city.

Additionally, the amount of middle-manager to director-level talent needed to support hyper growth companies of the Silicon Valley model is lacking in each of these cities. As such, many entrepreneurial ecosystem players throughout comeback cities see their development as a slower model built upon a mixture of venture capital-funded hyper growth startups and slower, more organic growth companies.

Another city that has seen recent success using their own model of startup ecosystem development is Birmingham, AL. An idea born out of Revolution's Rise of the Rest bus tour that visited Birmingham, this initiative seeks to bring companies to Birmingham as a potential second or third headquarter location. Chris Moody, a Partner at Foundry Group, has helped to lead this effort. Working with a group of local entrepreneurs along with support from Alabama Power and the City of Birmingham, the "Birmingham Bound" initiative serves to highlight everything the city can offer to a fast growth company.

The original Birmingham Bound company tour brought six companies from the Foundry Group portfolio, three of which have committed to opening a second location in Birmingham, with another cohort of companies in the works as I write this. Companies are shown the talent and resources that Birmingham can provide, many of which are similar to those offered by comeback cities. For instance, the city is home to the Innovation Depot, a 140,000 square foot facility that serves as a coworking space, an accelerator, and teaches courses for entrepreneurs. That depot currently houses 117 early stage startups and 1,200 people.

* * *

Another concept that has boomed in popularity in the past decade is one that could also be used in comeback city development. When I first heard the term "impact investing," I had no background on it, so I assumed it was basically synonymous with philanthropy. With impact having become a less-than-rigid buzzword to me by that point, I thought "Oh, if you're just looking to make an impact, it must just mean investing in social causes." In reality, adding the word impact to investing does not make it any less tangible; on the contrary, it serves to make investing far more meaningful to the masses. The concept of impact investing makes investing in comeback city redevelopment a worthwhile endeavor. If these cities can work to quantify and illustrate the impacts of investments in their redevelopment, the progress will accelerate rapidly.

The term impact investing was coined in 2007 as part of the Rockefeller Foundation's Impact Investing initiative. The leader of this initiative, Antony Bugg-Levine, describes the "bifurcated world" that most people inhabit as one in which they assume that "the only way to solve social challenges is through government and charity and that the only purpose of business and investing is to make money. Impact investors reject that worldview. We recognize that for-profit investment can be both a morally legitimate and economically effective way to address social and environmental challenges."[119]

Village Capital and Blueprint Local founder, Ross Baird, highlights the necessary change that impact investing brought to an investment world previously focused around the Silicon Valley model:

> *Most technology startups remain relevant only to the best-off in society, leaving out billions of people and trillion-dollar markets. Venture capitalists drive this mindset by avoiding industries with real-world impact — such as food, health and education — because they're capital-intensive, complicated and require serious regulatory engagement: "Health's too hard;" "the education sales cycles are too long."*[120]

These are precisely the industries that comeback cities can provide. There are considerable social and environmental challenges faced by comeback cities that undoubtedly would have an economic benefit that, if able to quantify, makes a worthy investment opportunity.

119 Kanani, Rahim. "The State and Future of Impact Investing". 2012. *Forbes*. https://www.forbes.com/sites/rahimkanani/2012/02/23/the-state-and-future-of-impact-investing/#f903249ed488

120 Baird, Ross. "We're at the Beginning of a Venture Capital Revolution". 2019. *Techcrunch*. https://techcrunch.com/2015/09/05/were-at-the-beginning-of-a-venture-capital-revolution/.

In many older cities across the country, including comeback cities, aging infrastructure poses considerable health threats. At the surface level, there is no financial play here, but if you consider the social, psychological, and productivity impacts of health concerns, this quickly becomes a worthy investment. For instance, children in Buffalo are at an increased risk of lead poisoning because of an older deteriorated housing stock and high rates of child poverty (53.9 percent in the city of Buffalo). Additionally, Buffalo Water estimates that sixty percent of city resident service lines running from the water main to the home contain lead. Although lead poisoning is harmful to all people, children are particularly susceptible to long-term effects, including loss of I.Q., developmental delays, learning disabilities, memory loss, hearing loss, attention deficits, hyperactivity, and behavioral disorders.[121] While the health impacts alone make it a worthwhile cause to replace these lines or find some alternative solution to the lead poisoning problem, replacement cost for each line averages $12,000, which would total approximately $500 million for all of the lines that contain lead.[122]

121 Gardner, Kent. "Renewing our Pledge: A Path to Ending Lead Poisoning of Buffalo's Most Vulnerable Citizens". 2017. *CGR*. https:// ppgbuffalo.org/files/documents/health/renewing_our_pledge__a_ path_to_ending_lead_poisoning_of_buffalos_most_vulnera- ble_citizens.pdf

122 Wolf, Anna. "Buffalo, NY: A Rust Belt City's New Approach to Tackling Lead in Drinking Water". 2019. *Center for Neighborhood Technology*. https://www.cnt.org/blog/buffalo-ny-a-rust-belt- city%E2%80%99s-new-approach-to-tackling-lead-in-drinking- water.

Taking an approach which quantifies the downstream economic effects of the potential health issues to children over the course of their life resulting from lead poisoning, the return on investment for a partnership solving this challenge becomes far more intriguing.

Another issue which is particularly trying in the regions surrounding comeback cities is the opioid epidemic. From an impact investment perspective, there are benefits in investing in direct solutions to the abuse and addiction issue itself, along with benefits from curbing the epidemic by investing in social determinants of health in these regions around comeback cities as a whole with the intention of reducing abuse and addiction by bettering these determinants. Beyond the human cost of 175 lives taken per day by the opioid crisis, not to mention the effects on those loved ones left behind, there are dramatic increases in hospitalizations and emergency room visits, increases in the number of babies born with neonatal abstinence syndrome, along with the innumerable impacts on productivity and economic activity of those both directly and indirectly affected by the abuse and addiction. The direct biotech solutions to address the crisis include alternative nonnarcotic painkiller development, pill packaging fixes, and support and accountability applications.

From a comeback city perspective, investment in social determinants of health can go a long way in preventing the continuation of the epidemic. At the highest level, economic prosperity positively benefits the social and psychological risk factors of the epidemic. A more specific example of a social determinant solution is to strengthen supports for public housing providers to avoid eviction of those for whom opioid addiction treatment is a possibility.[123] Although the annual economic cost of the crisis as a whole has been estimated at $193 million, being able to quantify the return of specific investments in building up comeback city cities and neighboring regions will attract investors to see the big picture results.[124]

Bugg-Levine stresses the importance of putting the concepts behind impact investing in their rightful place: "Impact investing is a tool, not an end in itself. If you approach the world asking 'where can I make an impact investment?' you will end up doing far less interesting work then if you ask 'what social challenges do I want to address, and how can impact investing be one of the tools I use to address them?'."[125]

123 Matthew, Dayna. 2018. "Un-Burying the Lead: Public Health Tools are the Key to Beating the Opioid Epidemic". *Brookings*. https://www.brookings.edu/research/un-burying-the-lead-public-health-tools-are-the-key-to-beating-the-opioid-epidemic/.

124 Bank, David. "Pain Killers: How Can Impact Investors Help Stop the Opioid Addiction Epidemic?". 2018. *Impact Alpha*. https://impactalpha.com/pain-killers-how-can-impact-investors-help-stop-the-opioid-addiction-epidemic/.

125 Kanani, Rahim. "The State and Future of Impact Investing". 2012. *Forbes*. https://www.forbes.com/sites/rahimkanani/2012/02/23/the-state-and-future-of-impact-investing/#f903249ed488

With the right mind-set, and a reframing of impact and return, comeback cities can become some of the most attractive areas to focus resources and attention for those involved in promoting and supporting entrepreneurship and economic growth.

The model will differ from city to city based on its available ecosystem components (universities, venture capitalists, etc.), meaning the only certainty in what this model will look like is that it should differ for each comeback city. Like Birmingham, each comeback city must think of creative ways to highlight its advantages.

Just like tourists and visitors tend to be won over by comeback cities once they give them a chance and see them firsthand, companies and investors will be impressed if each city's light is shined upon their best assets.

PART 5

EPILOGUE

CHAPTER 24

A PAGE FROM MOM'S BOOK

———

Skipping ahead looking to get a quick summary of the past however many pages? You've come to the wrong place.

There is no magic elixir. No politician that will draft a bill that will raise these cities from the dead with the wave of an arm like the Night King at Hardhome (fingers crossed this *Game of Thrones* reference is still relevant when you're reading this). No Google or Amazon that will Sim City in a new complex and complete the comeback of these cities.

The road will continue to twist for each of them. There will be plenty of new and unexpected obstacles. There will be barriers that have been looming in the distance for centuries that need to be broken down. How each city, each community, each company, each family, and each individual ultimately approaches these is yet to be determined.

If I were to present you with a foundational document for how each city can make strides towards its comeback, you would probably find it fluffy and meatless. What you may be looking for is a strategic plan which lays out tasks, responsibilities, milestones, and outcomes. I assure you there will be strategic plans laid out. And they will help us get there. But what really needs development is much bigger than that. Behavioral changes are the hardest to make, and in many cases the simplest to determine. And that's what we have before us.

If I were to boil it down to the simplest lesson of all that could have reverberating effects for the startup ecosystem of comeback cities and their broader communities, it is one that my mother would say to me on the way out the door to school every morning: "show kindness."

Stay with me here. It's simple, it's corny if you want to look at it that way, but it's all-encompassing.

I used to roll my eyes, give her a "Yeah, yeah, yeah" and be out the door. But now I see her say it to her grandkids, and my brothers say it to their own kids, and there are no more eye rolls from me. Only smiles. Because it seems to work.

If you know about startup ecosystem development, you know about the "give first" mentality. It is a mind-set in which you give with no expectation of anything in return, recognizing that at day's end a community rises and falls as one. Another tenant is to take risks and celebrate failures because even failures mark an earnest attempt at lessons learned.

These are must-haves for any good startup ecosystem, but to push beyond the core players in that ecosystem and have a city-wide rally around startups as an opportunity for economic, cultural, and communal growth, even those who don't see themselves as involved must adapt. Old boys' clubs in many comeback cities need to change the way they think about inclusion. Families in underserved parts of these cities and blue-collar workers from nearby suburbs all the way out to rural areas nearby need to recognize that they are welcome and necessary in this ecosystem too. It's not just a world built for computer programmers who play too much ping pong at work and can't be bothered to wear anything besides t-shirts, as many of those who have been excluded are led to believe.

An entrepreneur is anyone with an idea or a notion that must be embraced. So, even if these peripheral players don't know the finer points of startup tenants, the other-oriented nature of "show kindness" and "give first" is one thing everyone can adopt.

For comeback cities that were built long ago on innovation and have maintained themselves for many years simply on grit, there is a new day rising over the dilapidated grain elevators and steel mills.

* * *

Remember the story of One Seneca Tower, Buffalo's only skyscraper that was nearly ninety percent empty as of 2015? In the time it took me to write this book, one of Buffalo's largest corporations and employers (sustaining a local workforce of 7,500) M&T Bank has announced it will use the building to house its new tech hub. This lease agreement is not only a turning point for the 1.1 million-square-foot skyscraper, but it will also stand as a beacon to attract the 1,000+ technology professionals that M&T hopes to bring to the region as part of their technological transformation. So, as we mentioned, if a city's skyscraper(s) can be considered a representation of how they're doing, things are looking up in Buffalo.

Zombie tower, no more.[126]

No longer can each comeback city's grit be defined by its collective head staying down and its teeth clenching through another work day hoping for something to change. Instead,

---

126 Watson, Stephen & Glynn, Matt. 2019. "M&T Tech Hub and Its 1,000 Workers Headed to Buffalo's One Seneca Tower". *The Buffalo News*. https://buffalonews.com/2019/06/25/source-mt-to-locate-tech-hub-in-vacant-one-seneca-tower/.

these cities will be defined by a new, reimagined grit, where the people combine the toughness from lessons past with the selflessness and spirit necessary to build the city's future together and finally complete its comeback.

We're not just hoping, we're waiting.

.

ACKNOWLEDGEMENTS

———

Writing a book is a strange process filled with doubt, questions, and moments of temporary insanity. But most worthwhile endeavors are. I could not have finished this particular endeavor without a small army of support that I'm grateful for each and every day. To each of you who lent an ear, shared an opinion, showed your interest, or simply let me ramble on when the moment struck, thank you.

Thank you first and foremost to my family for supporting me through every step of the way, always: Mom, Dad, Matt, Shanna, Tom, Christian, Jon, Jen, Jack, Syd, Jimbo, Clare, Sean, Lucy, May, Will, Isla, Alec, Grandmother, aunts, uncles, and cousins by the dozens. Thank you to my Buffalo friends, Georgetown friends, Villanova friends, Pittsburgh friends, Baltimore friends, DC friends, startup community friends, and friends who have come into my life through any other lucky but unsorted act of good fortune.

Thank you to those who collaborated with me on this project, whether through formal interviews, research assistance, or offering their expertise: Steve Case, Brad Feld, Ian Hathaway, Jack Greco, Lesa Mitchell, Tom Gordon, Clark Dever, Mike Messore, Chris Heivly, Wendy Lea, Alex Krause Matlack, Catherine Bruns, Mark Rucci, Josh Schoop, Ian Sefferman, Tim Holcomb, Sheikh Shuvo, Aaron Watson, Justin Gutwein, Jeff Reid, Mike Leffer, Doan Winkel, Ashwin Puri, Colleen Heidinger, Alex Gress, Jenae Pitts, Sherry Linkon, Jack McGowan, Morris Wheeler, Ed Buchholz, Keith Alper, Mary Grove, Chris Moody, and Erik Pages.

And thank you to everyone who: gave me their time for a personal interview, pre-ordered the eBook, paperback, and multiple copies to make publishing possible, helped spread the word about *New Grit* to gather amazing momentum, and help me publish a book I am proud of. I am sincerely grateful for all of your help.

Adam Gutman	John Schichtel*
Alan Rosenhoch	Jon & Jen Gordon*
Alec Schappert	Jordan Hillman
Alex Berdahl	Jordan Weinberg
Alex Hanno	Joseph Smith*
Alex Matlack	Kate Huber
Alex Poulin	Kirsten Smith
Andrew Lentz	Kyle Hubbard*

Ben King	Lauren & Steve Orkis
Bernie Switzer	Lily Heil
Bob & Susie Schappert	Lindsay & Brian Friel
Caite Cutler	Lisa Smith
Caitlin Callahan	Liz Love
Caitlin Sullivan	Marc DiCroce
Cali Harris	Maria Ayers
Callie Wilkinson	Mark Rucci
Cameron Foley*	Mary Gordon
Cassandra Schappert*	Matt Bryan
Catherine Bruns	Matthew Glose*
Cathy & Rob Clifford	Matthew Midon*
Chong Hwan Kim	Michael DiRosa
Chris DeMarco*	Michael Hoerner
Chris Heivly	Michelle Wu
Danny Sunderland	Mike DeMarseilles
Darshan Shah	Natalie Hoerner
Deborah & Eric Kloss	Nicholas Hann
Dom Morgan*	Nolan Ahern
Drew Bassini	Omar Nazem*
Ed Buchholz	Peter Siderovski
Emily Neugold	Philip Hussey
Emily Piccione	Becca Richman
Eric Young	Rob Wilber
Estevan Astorga	Rohan Dalvi
Galo Bowen	Roudy Boursiquot
Gina LaPlante	Erika & Russ Burgstahler
Grace Bennett	Sam Golden
Gregory Jensen	Sania Mohammed*

Helen Schappert	Scott Wise
Hillary Hearns	Sean Gallahan*
Jack Greco*	Sheree Hillman
Jack McGowan	Thomas Gomboc
Jason Chang	Tom & Christian Gordon
Jessica Garay-Leano	Tom Godin
Jessica Piatek*	Tom & Colleen Schappert
Jim Dickey	Varun Premkumar
Jimmy Gordon*	Clark Dever
John Kappel	Zach Benfanti

Key: *multiple copies/campaign contributions

Finally, thank you to New Degree Press and my outstanding publishing and support team: Eric Koester, Brian Bies, Caitlin Panarella, Cynthia Tucker, Leila Summers, Bogna Brewczyk, and Gjorgji Pejkovski.

BIBLIOGRAPHY

———

"15 Charts That Show US VC Could Break Multiple Records In 2019".
2019. Pitchbook. https://pitchbook.com/news/articles/15-charts-that-show-us-vc-could-break-multiple-records-in-2019.

"39 North- St. Louis' New Agtech and Plant Science Innovation District". St. Louis Economic Development Partnership. 2019. https://stlpartnership.com/who-we-are/our-teams/39-north-agtech-district/.

"903: A New Way to Pay for College". 2019. Podcast. Planet Money.

Aberman, Jonathan, Erran Carmel, and Bini Byambasuren. 2019. "Cybersecurity Startup Founders in Greater Washington, DC". Kogod School of Business. https://www.american.edu/kogod/research/publications/upload/cyber_founders_report.pdf.

Agtmael, Antoine van, and Fred Bakker. 2018. *The Smartest Places on Earth: Why Rustbelts are the Emerging Hotspots of Global Innovation.* New York, NY: PublicAffairs.

Angier, Natalie. "Debate on Buildings: To Scrub or Not". 2019. *New York Times.* https://www.nytimes.com/1992/01/14/science/debate-on-buildings-to-scrub-or-not.html.

"Ann Arbor, Detroit Must Work Together to Further Investment, Rise of The Rest Panel Says". 2017. *Crain's Detroit Business.* https://www.crainsdetroit.com/article/20171012/news/641841/ann-arbor-detroit-must-work-together-to-further-investment-rise-of-the.

"AOL Founder Steve Case". 2019. Podcast. *Twenty Minute VC.*

"Assessment & Roadmap Report: Cleveland, OH". 2018. *Techstars Startup Community Development Program.*

Austin, John. 2018. "The Rust Belt Needs Capital to Turn Talent and Innovation into Jobs". *Brookings.* https://www.brookings.edu/blog/the-avenue/2018/08/14/the-rust-belt-needs-capital-to-turn-talent-and-innovation-into-jobs/.

Austrian, Ziona & Piazza, Merissa. 2014. "Barriers and Opportunities for Entrepreneurship in Older Industrial Regions". 215-243.

Babcock, Stephen. "Maryland Just Opened Up a Tax Credit for Cybersecurity Investors". 2018. Technical.ly Baltimore. https://technical.ly/baltimore/2018/09/13/maryland-opens-up-tax-credit-for-cybersecurity-investors/.

Baird, Ross. "We're at the Beginning of a Venture Capital Revolution". 2019. Techcrunch. https://techcrunch.com/2015/09/05/were-at-the-beginning-of-a-venture-capital-revolution/.

Bank, David. "Pain Killers: How Can Impact Investors Help Stop the Opioid Addiction Epidemic?". 2018. Impact Alpha. https://impactalpha.com/pain-killers-how-can-impact-investors-help-stop-the-opioid-addiction-epidemic/.

Bartley, Joshua. 2017. "Breaking Down the Delmar Divide". Nextstl. https://nextstl.com/2017/09/breaking-delmar-divide/.

Berube, Alan & Murray, Cecile. "Renewing America's economic promise through Older Industrial Cities". 2018. Brookings. https://www.brookings.edu/wp-content/uploads/2018/04/2018-04_brookings-metro_older-industrial-cities_full-report-berube_murray_-final-version_af4-18.pdf.

Bitar, Eric. "Why Pittsburgh is Ideal for Robotics Businesses". 2017. Robotics Business Review. https://www.roboticsbusinessreview.com/manufacturing/pittsburgh-ideal-robotics-businesses/.

Briggs, James. "Salesforce reorganization to shed workers in Indianapolis". 2018. Indianapolis Star. https://www.indystar.com/story/money/2018/08/06/salesforce-reorganization-shed-workers-indianapolis/914544002/.

Burton, Cindy. "Ford says it will spend $740M to bring Detroit train station project to life". Detroit Free Press. https://www.freep.com/story/money/business/2018/08/15/michigan-central-station-corktown-cost-740-million/994867002/

Buttigieg, Pete. 2015. "What If a City Has to Rethink Its Past To Understand Its Future?". Video. TEDxUND.

Campbell-Dollaghan, Kelsey. 2019. "Zombie Towers". Gizmodo. https://gizmodo.com/zombie-towers-5-vacant-or-foreclosed-skyscrapers-acros-1469650045.

"Carnegie Speech". Crunchbase. https://www.crunchbase.com/organization/carnegie-speech

Carpenter, Mackenzie & Todd, Deborah. "The Google Effect: How Has The Tech Giant Changed Pittsburgh's Commerce And Culture?". 2019. Pittsburgh Post-Gazette. https://www.post-gazette.com/business/tech-news/2014/12/07/Google-effect-How-has-tech-giant-changed-Pittsburgh-s-commerce-and-culture/stories/201412040291.

Case, Steve. 2016. *The Third Wave: An Entrepreneur's Vision of the Future. New York, NY: Simon and Schuster.*

Casselman, Ben. 2016. *"St. Louis is the New Startup Frontier". Fivethirtyeight. https://fivethirtyeight.com/features/st-louis-is-the-new-startup-frontier/.*

Casselman, Ben. 2019. *"Cities Hunt for Startup Magic". WSJ. https://www.wsj.com/articles/SB10001424127887324904004578539373656398096.*

Chavez, Lydia. *"Bethlehem Steel to Cut 7,300 Jobs at Upstate Plant". 1982. New York Times. https://www.nytimes.com/1982/12/28/business/bethlehem-steel-to-cut-7300-jobs-at-upstate-plant.html.*

Chinitz, Benjamin. 1961. *"Contrasts in Agglomeration: New York and Pittsburgh." The American Economic Review. 51, no. 2: 279-89. http://www.jstor.org/stable/1914493.*

Clifford, Catherine. 2018. *"Billionaire Mark Cuban: 'One of the Great Lies of Life is Follow Your Passions'". CNBC. https://www.cnbc.com/2018/02/16/mark-cuban-follow-your-passion-is-bad-advice.html.*

Constine, Josh. *"Facebook Acquires 'Mobile Technologies', Developer of Speech Translation App Jibbigo". 2013. Techcrunch. https://*

techcrunch.com/2013/08/12/facebook-acquires-mobile-technologies-speech-recognition-and-jibbigo-app-developer/.

"The Cool List 2018". 2019. National Geographic. https://www.nationalgeographic.co.uk/travel/2017/12/cool-list-2018.

Cooperman, Jeannette. 2014. "The Story Of Segregation In St. Louis". Stlmag. https://www.stlmag.com/news/the-color-line-race-in-st.-louis/.

Crowder, Nicole. 2015. "The Life and Slow Death of a Former Pennsylvania Steel Town". Washington Post. https://www.washingtonpost.com/news/in-sight/wp/2015/11/11/part-ii-the-life-and-slow-death-of-a-former-pennsylvania-steel-town/?noredirect=on.

"Detroit Homecoming Expats Invest in Their Hometown". 2019. Crain's Detroit Business. https://www.crainsdetroit.com/detroit-homecoming/detroit-homecoming-expats-invest-their-hometown.

Dewey, Caitlin. 2019. "Could This Be Buffalo's First Tech Goliath?". The Buffalo News. https://buffalonews.com/2019/05/10/acv-auctions-buffalo-from-the-bottom-to-1b-how-an-unsexy-startup-is-thriving-in-buffalo/.

Dienst, Jennifer. "Former Rust Belt Cities Rise Again as Innovation Hubs". 2019. PCMA. https://www.pcma.org/rust-belt-cities-re-invent-innovation-hubs-knowledge-economies/.

"DuoLingo". Crunchbase. https://www.crunchbase.com/organization/duolingo

"Economy". 2018. Encyclopedia of Cleveland History - Case Western Reserve University. https://case.edu/ech/articles/e/economy.

Engel, Jeff. "Scott Dorsey Reflects on ExacTtarget & the Rise of Indianapolis Tech". 2016. Xconomy. https://xconomy.com/indiana/2016/06/29/scott-dorsey-reflects-on-exacttar-get-the-rise-of-indianapolis-tech/.

Faberman, R. Jason. 2002. "Job Flows and Labor Dynamics in the U.S. Rust Belt". Monthly Labor Review.

Fang, Sara. "Accelerating Start-Up Ecosystems with the Power of 5". 2015. EY Consulting. https://consulting.ey.com/accelerating-start-up-ecosystems-with-the-%e2%80%9cpower-of-5%e2%80%9d/.

Faulk, Mike. 2017. "T-Rex Touts Thousands of Jobs, Millions of Dollars in Economic Output". St. Louis Dispatch. 2017. https://www.stltoday.com/business/local/t-rex-touts-thousands-of-jobs-millions-of-dollars-in/article_bd38bb9e-6672-53d7-b1e0-e319b587072e.html.

Feld, Brad, and David Kaplan. 2012. *Startup Communities: Building an Entrepreneurial Ecosystem in Your City*. Hoboken, NJ: John Wiley and Sons, Inc.

Florida, Richard. "High-Tech Startups are Still Concentrated in Just a Few Cities". 2017. *Citylab*. https://www.citylab.com/life/2017/10/venture-capital-concentration/539775/.

Florida, Richard. 2017. "Mapping America's 'Desperation Gap'". *Citylab*. https://www.citylab.com/life/2017/11/the-geography-of-desperation/545459/.

Foley, Aaron. "We Love Detroit, Even If You Don't". 2013. *Jalopnik*. https://jalopnik.com/we-love-detroit-even-if-you-dont-832204589.

Gallagher, Billy. 2013. "Marc Andreessen: The World Would Be Much Better If We Had 50 More Silicon Valleys". *Techcrunch*. https://techcrunch.com/2013/04/20/marc-andreessen-the-world-would-be-much-better-if-we-had-50-more-silicon-valleys/.

Gardner, Kent. "Renewing our Pledge: A Path to Ending Lead Poisoning of Buffalo's Most Vulnerable Citizens". 2017. *CGR*. https://ppgbuffalo.org/files/documents/health/renewing_our_pledge__a_path_to_ending_lead_poisoning_of_buffalos_most_vulnerable_citizens.pdf

"GDP By Metropolitan Area". 2019. U.S. Bureau of Economic Analysis (BEA). https://www.bea.gov/data/gdp/gdp-metropolitan-area.

Giffels, David. 2014. The Hard Way on Purpose. New York: Scribner.

Glaeser, Edward, and Jacob Vigdor. 2012. "The End of the Segregated Century: Racial Separation in America's Neighborhoods, 1890–2010". Manhattan Institute CSLL Civic Report, no. 66.

Glaeser, Edward, Sari Kerr, and William Kerr. 2012. "Entrepreneurship and Urban Growth: An Empirical Assessment with Historical Mines". NBER Working Paper Series. National Bureau of Economic Research.

Graham, Tim. 2019. "'Siberian' Stigma: How the Bills Recruit Free Agents To...". The Athletic. https://theathletic.com/790400/2019/01/29/siberian-stigma-how-the-bills-recruit-free-agents-to-buffalo-and-why-deep-pockets-dont-always-help/.

Harrison, Jill. "Rust Belt Boomerang: The Pull of Place in Moving Back to a Legacy City". 2017. City & Community. https://www.researchgate.net/publication/319104431_Rust_Belt_Boomerang_The_Pull_of_Place_in_Moving_Back_to_a_Legacy_City

Hathaway, Ian. 2017. "Feeling Isolated? Build a Diaspora". Ian Hathaway. http://www.ianhathaway.org/blog/2017/6/6/feeling-isolated-build-a-diaspora?rq=diaspora.

Henderson, Tom. "Heavyweight Investors Join Dan Gilbert in New VC Fund in Detroit". 2016. Crain's Detroit Business. https://www.crainsdetroit.com/article/20160111/NEWS/160119974/heavy-weight-investors-join-dan-gilbert-in-new-vc-fund-in-detroit.

Hensel, Anna. 2017. "Jeff Bezos, Eric Schmidt, and Others Give $150 Million to Steve Case's Middle America Startup Fund". Venturebeat. https://venturebeat.com/2017/12/04/jeff-bezos-eric-schmidt-and-others-give-150-million-to-steve-cases-middle-america-startup-fund/.

Hensel, Anna. 2018. "How Salesforce's Acquisition of ExactTarget Helped Indianapolis' Tech Community Flourish". Venturebeat. https://venturebeat.com/2018/07/01/how-salesforces-acquisition-of-exacttarget-helped-indianapolis-tech-community-flourish/.

Hensel, Anna. 2018. "Indianapolis' Highalpha Raises Over $100 Million For Its Enterprise Software-Focused 'Venture Studio'". Venturebeat. https://venturebeat.com/2018/07/16/indianapolis-highalpha-raises-over-100-million-for-its-enterprise-software-focused-venture-studio/.

"High Alpha Raises Over $100M to Launch High Alpha Studio II and High Alpha Capital II". 2018. High Alpha. https://highalpha.com/introducing-high-alpha-ii/.

Hopson, Chris. 2018. "The Draw of Consulting and Finance". Harvard Political Review. http://harvardpolitics.com/harvard/the-draw-of-consulting-and-finance/.

Hudson, Marc. "Detroit's Broadband Infrastructure". 2015. FCC. http://transition.fcc.gov/c2h/10282015/marc-hudson-presentation-10282015.pdf

"Imagining the World's First Cancer Center". 2019. Roswell Park Comprehensive Cancer Center. https://www.roswellpark.org/cancertalk/201803/imagining-worlds-first-cancer-center.

"The Importance of Young Firms for Economic Growth". 2014. Entrepreneurship Policy Digest. Kauffman Foundation.

"Imported from Detroit: Shinola Settles into Taubman Center". 2012. Curbed Detroit. https://detroit.curbed.com/2012/8/7/10343488/imported-from-detroit-shinola-introduces-neomanufacturing-to-detroit#more.

Kanani, Rahim. "The State and Future of Impact Investing". 2012. Forbes. https://www.forbes.com/sites/rahimkanani/2012/02/23/the-state-and-future-of-impact-investing/#f903249ed488

Kane, Tim. 2010. "The Importance of Startups in Job Creation and Job Destruction". Kauffman Foundation Research Series: Firm Formation and Economic Growth. Kauffman Foundation.

Kennedy, Patrick. "Nonprofit Plugs Twin Cities Teens into Silicon Valley Tech". 2018. Star Tribune. http://www.startribune.com/twin-cities-team-tackle-silicon-valley-during-tech-camp/490027101/.

Koenig, Neil. "Secret of Silicon Valley's Success". 2014. BBC News. https://www.bbc.com/news/technology-26041341.

Kosten, Dan. "Immigrants as Economic Contributors: Immigrant Entrepreneurs". 2018. National Immigration Forum. https://immigrationforum.org/article/immigrants-as-economic-contributors-immigrant-entrepreneurs/.

Lancee, Bram, and Herman G. Van de Werfhorst. 2012. "Income Inequality And Participation: A Comparison Of 24 European Countries". Social Science Research 41 (5): 1166-1178. doi:10.1016/j.ssresearch.2012.04.005.

Levingston, Chelsey. "Chiquita Gets $22 Million To Move Headquarters to Charlotte ". 2011. Dayton Daily News. https://www.daytondailynews.com/news/local/chiquita-gets-million-move-headquarters-charlotte/S7ayK3KcL8pSihJm573j3H/.

Linkon, S. (2018). The Half-life of Deindustrialization. Ann Arbor: University of Michigan Press, p.4.

Lohr, Steve. "Midwest Beckons Tech Investors". 2017. New York Times. https://www.nytimes.com/2017/11/19/technology/midwest-tech-startups.html.

MacDonald, Christine. "Detroiters' income rises for second year but poverty rate doesn't improve". 2018. The Detroit News. https://www.detroitnews.com/story/news/local/detroit-city/2018/09/13/census-detroiters-income-rise/1268641002/.

Marcus, Jon. 2010. Times Higher Education. http://www.higheredu-cation.org/crosstalk/ctbook/pdfbook/OhioBrainDrainBookLay-out.pdf

Matthew, Dayna. 2018. "Un-Burying the Lead: Public Health Tools are the Key to Beating the Opioid Epidemic". Brookings. https://www.brookings.edu/research/un-burying-the-lead-public-health-tools-are-the-key-to-beating-the-opioid-epidemic/.

McNamer, Bruce & Zeuli, Kim. "Cities Need Small Business Growth Strategies". 2019. JPMC City Makers. https://www.theatlantic.com/sponsored/jpmc-city-makers/cities-need-small-business-growth-strategies/149/.

Morelix, Arnobio, and Josh Russell-Fritch. 2017. "Kauffman Index of Growth Entrepreneurship". Kauffman Foundation. https://www.kauffman.org/kauffman-index/reporting/-/media/e37f4200462347dbb0d385e01e656be2.ashx.

Moutzalias, Tanya. "Early 1900s Photos Show the Early Years of the Detroit Auto Show". 2018. Mlive. https://www.mlive.com/news/detroit/2018/01/historic_photos_of_the_detroit.html.

Nash-Hoff, Michele. 2016. "Cincinnati's Cintrifuse Connects Entre-preneurs, Big Companies and Tech Funds". Industry Week. https://www.industryweek.com/innovation/cincinnatis-cintri-fuse-connects-entrepreneurs-big-companies-and-tech-funds.

"Next Things Now: Innovation & Entrepreneurship In Buffalo". 2019. YouTube. https://www.youtube.com/watch?v=E-YgcN-en3U.

O'Brien, Barbara, and The News. 2016. "Nation's First Gas Well Was Dug In Western New York". The Buffalo News. https://buffalonews.com/2016/10/12/nations-first-gas-well-dug-buffa-los-backyard/.

Obschonka, M., Schmitt-Rodermund, E., Silbereisen, R. K., Gosling, S. D., & Potter, J. 2013. "The regional distribution and correlates of an entrepreneurship-prone personality profile in the United States, Germany, and the United Kingdom: A socioecological perspective". Journal of Personality and Social Psychology.

Obschonka, Martin. "Research: The Industrial Revolution Left Psy-chological Scars that Can Still be Seen Today". 2018. Harvard Business Review. https://hbr.org/2018/03/research-the-industrial-revolution-left-psychological-scars-that-can-still-be-seen-today.

"Overview". 2019. Silicon North Stars Youth Program. http://www. siliconnorthstars.org/overview/.

Pare, Mike. "Moving Fast: The Freight Services Sector is Riding High in Chattanooga, 'The Silicon Valley Of Trucking'". 2019. Chattanooga Times Free Press. https://www.timesfreepress.com/ news/edge/story/2019/oct/01/moving-fast-freight-services-sector-riding-hi/504428/.

"Popular Cities in America: Where People are Moving to Fastest ". 2016. ABODO Apartments. https://www.abodo.com/blog/ so-long-to-the-city/.

Reel, Monte. 2018. "The Irresistible Urge to Build Cities from Scratch". Bloomberg Businessweek. https://www.bloomberg.com/news/ features/2018-11-02/the-irresistible-urge-to-build-cities-from-scratch.

Rushe, Dominic. 2017. "End of the Road: Will Automation Put an End To the American Trucker?". The Guardian. https://www. theguardian.com/technology/2017/oct/10/american-trucker-automation-jobs.

Saunders, Pete. "Detroit: America's Newest Tech Hub". 2019. Forbes. https://www.forbes.com/sites/petesaunders1/2017/02/15/ detroit-americas-newest-tech-hub/#c899d129faf1.

Saxenian, AnnaLee. 2007. *The New Argonauts: Regional Advantage in a Global Economy*. Harvard University Press.

Schuyler, David, and Bill Cieslewicz. 2018. "Milwaukee Ranks Among Best Cities to Start a Business". *Milwaukee Business Journal*. https://www.bizjournals.com/milwaukee/news/2018/12/26/milwaukee-ranks-among-best-cities-to-start-a.html.

Segedy, Jason. 2018. "Why are Some People in the Rust Belt So Resistant to Change?". *Cleveland Scene*. https://www.clevescene.com/scene-and-heard/archives/2018/12/07/why-are-some-people-in-the-rust-belt-so-resistant-to-change.

Senor, Dan, and Saul Singer. 2011. *Start-Up Nation*. Toronto: McClelland & Stewart.

Serrat, Olivier. "The Five Whys Technique". *Knowledge Solutions*. Singapore: Springer.

Smarsh, Sarah. "Something Special is Happening in Rural America". 2019. *New York Times*. https://www.nytimes.com/2019/09/17/opinion/rural-america.html?smid=nytcore-ios-share.

"Techstars and 43North Partner to Grow Entrepreneurial Ecosystem in Buffalo". 2019. *Techstars Blog*. https://www.techstars.com/content/accelerators/techstars-43north-partner-grow-entrepreneurial-ecosystem-buffalo/.

"Techstars' Brad Feld: A Startup Community Needs a 20-Year Time Horizon". 2013. Podcast. Knowledge@Wharton. https://knowledge.wharton.upenn.edu/article/techstars-brad-feld-a-startup-community-needs-a-20-year-time-horizon/.

Teicher, Jordan. "Millennials are Moving to Buffalo & Living Like Kings". 2015. Gothamist. https://gothamist.com/news/millennials-are-moving-to-buffalo-living-like-kings.

"Topophilia". 2019. Stamps School of Art and Design. https://stamps.umich.edu/exhibitions/detail/topophilia.

"Unequal Stress: How Poverty is Toxic for Children's Brains". 2016. Mailman School of Public Health. https://www.mailman.columbia.edu/public-health-now/news/unequal-stress-how-poverty-toxic-children%E2%80%99s-brains.

Upbin, Bruce. "Salesforce to Buy ExactTarget for $2.5 Billion". 2013. Forbes. https://www.forbes.com/sites/bruceupbin/2013/06/04/salesforce-to-buy-exacttarget-for-2-5-billion/#77a79e84cfcc.

VanAntwerp, Tom. "The Real Value of $100 in Metropolitan Areas". 2015. Tax Foundation. https://taxfoundation.org/real-value-100-metropolitan-areas-0.

Wagner, Allen. "The Venture Capital Lifecycle". 2014. Pitchbook. https://pitchbook.com/news/articles/the-venture-capital-life-cycle.

Walker, Melody. 2018. "Brookings Report: St. Louis' Economy Doing Better Than Many Older Industrial Cities". Stl Public Radio. https://news.stlpublicradio.org/post/brookings-report-st-lou-is-economy-doing-better-many-older-industrial-cities#stream/0.

Warren, Tamara. "Inside Detroit's Crumbling Train Station That Ford Plans to Transform into a Mobility Lab". 2018. The Verge. https://www.theverge.com/2018/6/20/17483696/ford-detroit-train-station.

Watson, Stephen & Glynn, Matt. 2019. "M&T Tech Hub and Its 1,000 Workers Headed to Buffalo's One Seneca Tower". The Buffalo News. https://buffalonews.com/2019/06/25/source-mt-to-locate-tech-hub-in-vacant-one-seneca-tower/.

Weissmann, Eric. "Creating an Ecosystem: Who Benefits When Big Companies Work With Startups?". 2018. Forbes. https://www.forbes.com/sites/forbescommunicationscouncil/2018/08/14/creating-an-ecosystem-who-benefits-when-big-compa-nies-work-with-startups/#6c46cd12539f.

West, Rebecca & Gast, Jenn. "Port Covington Set to Become a Global Cybersecurity Hub". 2019. PRWEB. https://www.prweb.com/